What people are saying about

Hope From Heaven

Hope From Heaven is a candid, very intimate account of the spiritual events in the author's life. Ranging from a near-death experience (NDE) at 14 to her appointment as God's messenger, and having had numerous after-death (ADC) experiences, Elissa Hope has led a very rich and blessed life.
Bill Guggenheim, co-author of *Hello From Heaven!*

Hope From Heaven will not only take your breath away but inspire you to breathe life in more deeply. Elissa Hope reminds you through this magical story that by connecting with your loved one's spirit you will feel that deep sense of love and connection that never ends. A truly inspiring book!
Sunny Dawn Johnston, psychic, medium, angel communicator and author of *Invoking the Archangels* and *The Love Never Ends*

I endorse the truth and so definitely endorse Elissa's book *Hope From Heaven*. I have been there and can accept the truth and realize what is true and not controversial as I was called decades ago. *Hope From Heaven* is a real page-turner and beautifully written, so read and learn and be prepared to meet your truth and angels.
Dr. Bernie Siegel, *New York Times* bestselling author of *Love, Medicine and Miracles* and *Peace, Love and Healing*

Elissa Hope has written a phenomenal book about her near-death experience as a teenager and its impact
From deep within her heart, Elissa
story that allows a deeper understa
lessons that all is not always what

This terrific page-turner reads like a romance novel; however, don't let it fool you. There are many spiritual truths shared. The triumphs and sorrows that led to her personal transformation are steeped in the energy of God's unconditional love and remembering the Angels' messages. Like most young girls she yearned for her soul mate. Finally she found her way to Todd by listening to the Angelic Kingdom. However, the story does not end there. *Hope From Heaven* is a great read that explores endless love and how to embrace God's healing light.

Monique Chapman, intuitive consultant and host of, *Get Over It!* Podcast

Hope From Heaven

A True Story Of Divine Intervention
And The Girl Who Came Back
As God's Messenger

Hope From Heaven

A True Story Of Divine Intervention
And The Girl Who Came Back
As God's Messenger

Elissa Hope

BOOKS

Winchester, UK
Washington, USA

JOHN HUNT PUBLISHING

First published by O-Books, 2023
O-Books is an imprint of John Hunt Publishing Ltd., 3 East St., Alresford,
Hampshire SO24 9EE, UK
office@jhpbooks.com
www.johnhuntpublishing.com
www.o-books.com

For distributor details and how to order please visit the 'Ordering' section on our website.

Text copyright: Elissa Hope 2022

ISBN: 978 1 80341 174 3
978 1 80341 175 0 (ebook)
Library of Congress Control Number: 2022931296

A CIP catalogue record for this book is available from the British Library.

Design: Stuart Davies

UK: Printed and bound by CPI Group (UK) Ltd, Croydon, CR0 4YY
Printed in North America by CPI GPS partners

We operate a distinctive and ethical publishing philosophy in all areas of our business, from our global network of authors to production and worldwide distribution.

Contents

To my precious daughter, Raphaela,
who is the wind beneath my wings
and Todd, my eternal Twin Flame

Acknowledgements

First and foremost I thank God for making this book *Hope From Heaven* possible. It has been forty years in the making, and a dream come true! I thank God for all of my incredible blessings and for sending me back to my life with such an important purpose. It has been quite a journey that has led me to writing my inspirational memoir *Hope From Heaven*. This book is dedicated to Todd, and in Honor of God. It is a Tribute to Todd and my Legacy.

Thank you to my Beloved Twin Flame Todd Irvin, my precious Twin Soul: you are in me, with me, and a part of me always. I cherish all of your extraordinary afterlife communication with me. Thank you for guiding me from heaven to complete our Twin Flames mission together.

Thank you to my Lovely Guardian Angels for all of your unconditional love, unwavering support, protection, and guidance. You told me years ago if I continue to work hard on my writing, and never give up that I will be very successful at it one day. Thank you for all of your encouragement. It is your inspiring words that kept me going and led me to getting my book published. You are my guiding light!

A big thank you to everyone on my publishing team at John Hunt Publishing O-Books. Dominic James, Gavin Davies, Stuart Davies, Charlotte Edwards, Krystina Kellingley, Steve Wagstaff, Nick Welch, Mary Flatt, Frank Smecker, Elizabeth Radley. And, a very special thank you to O-Books commissioner Michael Mann, who believed in me and my book from day one. Michael, you are not only my mentor, but a real friend!

Thank you to my mother who has always been my biggest cheerleader, and cheering me on from the sidelines each and every single day since I started writing this book.

Another special thank you to my beautiful daughter Raphaela

for being the amazing daughter that you are! Your love and support throughout this whole endeavor are beyond words!

Thank you to my brother Brad for all of your wonderful advice, and to my sister-in-law Adrienne who was always there to lend an ear. And to my two nieces Leah and Adina. Thank you for all of your encouragement! Thank you to my cousin Susan, and Joe for all of your love and support!

Thank you to Rick Garside, and Karen Covell for being such a wonderful mentor and friend.

Thank you to Dwight Woodward for all of your kind words. They mean so much to me!

Thank you to all of my friends who have always been there for me and offered so many words of wisdom. Susan, Casey, Mary, Rhonda, Jody, Gloria, Trish, Kaitlin, Katherine, Lisa, Christine, and best friend Susie—I truly know the meaning of sisterhood because of all of you!

Thank you to Ellen, Tom, Carolyn, Scott, Suzy, and Nora at the Cold Spring Harbor Library. And many thanks to Christine at CSH Jr./Sr. HS, Chairperson of Art. Christine, you have such a big heart! I am so appreciative of all of your support!

Thank you to Anne Barthel who I consider not just an editor but a friend as well.

With appreciation to Bruce Weber, who encouraged me to write this book!

A special thank you to Sunny Dawn Johnston, Monique Chapman, Dr. Bernie Siegel, and Bill Guggenheim for endorsing my book! And, my deepest gratitude to Dr. Harmony for writing such an inspirational foreword!

Foreword

Warning: This book may inspire, impact and influence your perception of how you might get to Heaven and who might "show up" in your life to usher you through the pearly gates.

Society teaches us that Heaven exists in the sky somewhere upon a cloud and is a resting place where we wait to experience the hereafter.

Hope From Heaven offers a new perspective on where you go when you die. It will enlighten you with peace and is a living testament to the idea that you have already planned out the destiny of your life. Therefore, you can rest at ease, knowing everything is happening in Divine order.

Elissa leads you by the hand and heart in this book as she shares her near-death experience. You can feel her dedication to her mission. Her message is to help others turn life challenges into a conquest the same way she did. And she will leave you applauding her victory.

Furthermore, this messenger from Heaven offers hope, as she reveals the excruciating pain she encountered throughout her twin-flame ascension journey. She will captivate you with love, humility, and humor as the pages unfold.

Elissa's story exemplifies that your path is your purpose, and when you turn your tragedy into a triumph, it becomes the gift back. Know that your message can bring hope to others.

She has endured many challenges and has achieved the self-mastery required to receive the keys that unlocked the enlightenment gateway, allowing her to experience Heaven on earth in her daily walk through life. To gather such expertise, a person has to undergo great sorrow and suffering before embodying the depths of Universal love.

Before we are born, we create agreements with the soul family that agree to facilitate our self-actualization and learn lessons for our spiritual evolution. These interactions with others cause us to experience painful and difficult situations. They teach us to transcend limiting beliefs, generational curses, cultural conditions, and toxic relationships, and to reprogram old patterns that no longer serve our purpose. This process is known as ascension.

The ascension journey assists us in letting go of who we have been, learning to love who we are, and embracing who we are becoming. The purpose of this transformative rebirth and metamorphosis is to help us rise above our limitations and regenerate into the best version of who we came here to earth to be.

When our soul is ready to reach these higher states of consciousness, we experience a dark night before we can discover the light of God inside ourselves. This intense quest assists the soul to align with all aspects of oneself and become whole—prepared to return to oneness with its other half.

Around this time, your twin flame might "show up" in your life to become your most remarkable mirrored reflection, helping you see, feel and heal the deepest sides of yourself. They will activate you to accelerate your ascension, helping expose your shadows so you can purify and free your soul from past karmic experiences.

Your twin flame is the other half of you. Coming together is magnetic and gives you a feeling of being home because they make you feel "whole" again. They enter your life to help you discover your authentic self as you learn to accept, forgive and find compassion for your emotional wounds.

Like a soul mate, you may feel like you have known them forever. You only have one twin flame. You and your twin flame may have similar characteristics that parallel. In addition, your differences tend to complement each other like yin and yang.

Both twin flames must have personally developed and spiritually evolved to accomplish inner balance before they can harmonize and experience a rhythm that keeps them as one unified unit.

Coming into alignment with your twin flame is intense and overwhelming, because you may feel like you constantly have to face the sides of yourself that you have suppressed. This push-pull effect can lead to separation, also known as a runner-chaser dynamic. Ultimately, your twin flame will teach you to love yourself before you can experience the ultimate relationship with your beloved.

Accomplishing soul mastery is required to reunite with your twin flame and become one. It used to be less than a 1% chance that you would incarnate during the same lifetime as your twin flame, much less reunite with them.

Today, we are an awakening planet with a collective mission to restore Heaven on earth — a place of inner peace and happiness. That is why more twin flames in the history of time are waking up to their identity to fulfill a self-**LOVE** r**EVOL**ution.

You and your twin flame have an unbreakable bond, because twin flames are meant to be together for eternity. Together they have a joint mission with the intention of bringing higher states of love from Heaven to earth.

Twin flames are the "chosen ones" who signed up for the earth school assignment of redefining relationships. They are messengers of God and have a collective mission to bring higher states of love from Heaven to earth.

Elissa and Todd were proficient ascension students, allowing them to align physically and share twin flame love — the greatest love known to humankind. However, not all twin flames agreed to live in the same dimension — and in their case, not for an extended time. Together, their higher selves decided to pay the ultimate sacrifice of separating from this earth plane, creating a bigger mission than they could have accomplished by staying on the physical dimension together.

This act of unconditional love is the same Christ-conscious sacrifice Jesus made when he chose to ascend back to Heaven, leaving a legacy of light that showed people how to find their truth and discover their way back towards Heaven.

As a twin-flame ascension expert, I have assisted thousands of twin flames from Hollywood to Bollywood who have awakened to their identity in the masses. All were in search of clarity to understand why they are going through the pitfalls of hell. I offer them a better understanding of the reason they are experiencing such sorrow and suffering. I help them release their past, raise their consciousness and reclaim their power so they can share Heaven on earth—a place of inner peace and happiness.

Hope From Heaven is a Divine message that Elissa's soul was assigned to deliver to the world as part of her and Todd's twin-flame mission. I can assure you she has honored her higher conscious agreement by putting her pain into a purpose so that you, the reader, can learn from her experiences. She brings you *Hope From Heaven* to find inner peace and happiness in your daily life.

I know that God, her twin-flame angel Todd, her grandmother Lily, Shag, Frankie, and many others are in Heaven smiling down on her. They are all proud of her and high-fiving each other in a celebration because she has accomplished the mission.

And from one Divine messenger to another, Elissa, God gave me this message to share with you... Well done, my good and faithful servant, you have brought *Hope From Heaven!*

It is done—It is done—It is done.

And so it is...
And so it be...

PS...
Happy Valentine's Day, My Darling Elissa
Love, Your Angel Todd

Dr. Harmony
Twin Flame Ascension Expert & Quantum Healer
Author of *Twin Flame Code Breaker*

Prologue

"What is it, my child? Why are you so upset? Why are you crying?"

Those were the most amazing words that I had ever heard, because I knew that they were coming directly out of the mouth of God. You know when you hear the saying "from your mouth to God's ears"? This time I knew for sure that God had heard my call for him, because he was standing right in front of me.

Part I

Meeting God

Chapter 1

A Trip to the Dentist

As we drove down Long Beach Road toward the shopping center, I was thinking how pretty the ground looked, with so many different colors of leaves decorating the sidewalks. Never in my young teenage years did I think I was going to die that day. After all, I was only fourteen, too young to know much about death, and definitely too young to die. But God had different plans for me. He needed me back in heaven, at least for a little bit. On that chilly November afternoon in 1981, a few days before Thanksgiving, my mother had picked me up from school early. While the rest of my ninth-grade classmates were still writing down their homework assignments, she was taking me to the dentist to have a cavity filled, and then we were going to the supermarket to stock up for the holiday meal. Thanksgiving was a big family party, with my mother and father, my two older brothers, and my grandparents, whom I loved. Especially my grandmother, Lily—I thought she was the best grandmother in the world. In our little town of Oceanside, a close-knit community on the South Shore of Long Island where pretty much everyone knew pretty much everyone else, everyone loved Lily. Her smile and her laughter could light up any room she was in.

Some kids hate going to the dentist's office, but I had no problem with the dentist. In fact, now that I had finally got my braces off my teeth, I felt reasonably happy about the dental profession! Along with my new straight pearly-white smile, I had just signed a contract with a modeling agency. Modeling was a whole new world to me, and it was very exciting to get to take off of school sometimes and go into New York City on "go-sees" with different agencies and clients. Sometimes, when you looked around the room and saw a hundred other pretty girls all there for the same job, it could shake your confidence, but I always told myself, if it's meant to be, it will be. And it was very exciting when I actually did land a job. At five feet six inches, I wasn't tall enough to do runway modeling, but I did have thick, wavy blonde hair that all the kids at school admired. My hair was my trademark. Clairol had picked my picture off the wall at the agency, and I had started doing hair shows for them. Once, at a show, a hairdresser who worked with Farrah Fawcett said, "I finally met someone who has more hair than Farrah!" (Remember, this was 1981.) I also did some catalog work for stores like Macy's, Bloomingdale's and Saks Fifth Avenue, and I had just appeared in a commercial for Huckapoo shirts that my best friend, Amy, and I stayed up half the night to watch on TV. Amy was like a sister to me, maybe because I'd always wanted one; I only had the two older brothers. My mother wanted a daughter so badly, but when she gave birth to me, she didn't believe the doctor when he said it was a girl. She was still groggy from the anesthesia, and she kept saying, "I don't believe you—it's another boy, I know it." Finally the doctor pulled my diaper off and said, "Look!" Then my mother screamed so loud she almost burst doctor's eardrum.

Sometimes it's true that the apple doesn't fall far from the tree. My mother and I had the same irrepressible sense of humor—she'd been the class clown, just like me—and she had modeled herself when she was younger, so she was very supportive about my newfound career. We had always been close, and now we had this in common too. So I wasn't sitting there sulking as we drove along, or arguing with my mom, or trying to pretend she didn't exist, the way some teenagers would. I was much too easygoing for that. I didn't even mind that we were going to a different dentist this time. My mother said she was about to spend a fortune in the supermarket buying the turkey and all the trimmings for everyone who was coming over, so she wanted to save a little money by taking me to a dental clinic that had just opened up at the Times Square shopping center in Oceanside, a big mall that was a hangout for all the local teenagers. TSS, as we called it, had everything under one roof, even a pet store. Being the easygoing teen that I was, I said, "Sure, Mom, no problem." I figured what did it matter which dentist I went to? I just wanted to get it over with.

Anyway, I had other things to think about. The holiday season was about to kick off, and this was my favorite time of year, when I always found myself in the festive holiday spirit. Where my mother was taking me to have my cavity filled was pretty much of no concern to me. I was starting to wrap my brain around all the presents I needed to start buying for my friends for Christmas and Hanukkah. My junior high school was so diverse that it was pretty much a tie—half my friends were Jewish and the other half were Christian, which suited me just fine. I never paid much attention to religion. We celebrated the big holidays, and I was bat mitzvahed, because that was what you did if you were Jewish and thirteen, but my family had probably not gone to temple once since then.

I did always believe strongly in God, though. Ever since I was a very young girl I had always said a prayer to God every morning and again every night. I knew from a very tender age that without God, none of us would be here. My prayer to God was exactly the same every day, day in and day out, and it went as follows: *Dear God, thank you for the precious gift of life. Please keep me and my family healthy, safe, and protected, and please let* (whichever boy I happened to have a crush on at the time) *ask me out. Thank you, amen.* I guess that would be a pretty typical prayer for a fourteen-year-old girl! Over the years, I'm proud to say, my prayers have changed quite a bit. You know how when you're a teenager, you think you know the ways of the world, and then when you become a grown-up, you realize just how little you really knew and how much you had to learn? Well, I was no exception to that rule. I definitely thought that I knew it all. I had no idea how much my horizons were about to expand. Or maybe I had some inkling after all, because as we were pulling into the parking lot, I turned to my mom. "Are you sure this is a good dentist?" "Yeah, sure," she said. "How bad can he be?"

We parked the car and went inside. The waiting room was very plain and pretty empty. It smelled a little like paint, I guess because the place was new, but when I looked at the magazines on the table, they were all old, just like in my other dentist's office. Maybe dentists had someplace they went to buy old magazines cheap. I didn't have time to read them anyway. I filled out some paperwork and a couple of minutes later I was lying back in the dentist's chair.

He came in and introduced himself—an ordinary-looking man with thick dark hair and not much else to notice about him. Maybe I would have noticed more if I'd known he might be the last person I would ever see! He asked me what kind of anesthetic I wanted, Novocain or nitrous oxide, otherwise known as laughing gas. What teenager wouldn't opt for the laughing gas? I had had it before and never had a problem, so I thought nothing of it now. "Don't worry," the dentist said. "I'm going to give you so much that you won't feel a thing." I thought that was a little odd, and as I looked at him more closely, I started to feel uneasy. He looked a little glassy-eyed to me, and I thought his pupils were dilated. There was even something funny in the way he moved. I wondered if perhaps he had given himself a little whiff of that stuff too! Now I was getting a very creepy feeling—I guess you could call it a bad vibe—and starting to wish I was at my regular dentist after all. I made a mental note to tell my mother not to bring me here again. At my regular dentist's office, there was a diploma up on every wall. Looking around, I realized there were no diplomas on these walls at all. The dentist came around the chair. "Here's the good stuff," he said. Then he covered my face with the mask, and that was the last I remembered.

Chapter 2

Through the Tunnel and Into the Light

I found myself moving through a long speeding tunnel. The best way I can describe it is like hearing the sound of wind on the windiest day. It was a loud whooshing sound that went on and on as I traveled through that tunnel at great speed for what seemed a very long time. I remember thinking, *Am I ever going to come out of this tunnel? And where am I going?* I knew it was definitely to a place I had never been before, as this tunnel seemed very out of the ordinary to me. The only other tunnel I had ever been in was the one that leads you into New York City, and this was surely not that tunnel, because I was not in a car! *Where are all the cars?* I wondered. My next thought was that maybe I was on a train and it was going to pull into Grand Central Station at any moment. But I think I somehow understood that I had left my body behind, and this was one journey my soul was taking on its own. All this time, my mother was sitting in the dentist's waiting room going over the Thanksgiving shopping list. The supermarket was right there in the same shopping center with the dental clinic, which made it very convenient for her, and we were going to go there after my cavity was filled. Little did she know what was really going on in the examining room! Never in her wildest dreams could she have imagined that her only daughter had just died in the dentist's chair. What had happened, I found out later, was this: the dentist had given me too much nitrous oxide, and it cut off my oxygen supply. I stopped breathing, I had no pulse, and I was clinically dead. I'm sure if my mother knew this could happen, she would have skipped the turkey and all the trimmings and taken me to my regular dentist instead! Well, you live and you learn, and as they say, what doesn't kill you can only make you stronger.

Unfortunately, this poor judgment on my mother's part *did* kill me. I can just imagine the scene that was unfolding in the dentist's chair. That incompetent wack-a-doodle dentist, hell-bent on pumping his patients (and probably himself too) full of laughing gas, now had a very serious matter on his hands. By this time I'm sure he realized what had happened, and he was frantically trying to revive me with CPR, all the while having visions of losing his license (if he had one in the first place) and even going to jail.

Sometimes ignorance definitely is bliss; to this day my mother says it's a good thing she did not know what had happened until after I came back to life, as she is sure she would have had a heart attack on the spot. Now, forty years later, as the mother of an only daughter myself, I understand one hundred percent where she is coming from. I don't think I would survive anything like that happening to my daughter. If I didn't drop dead of a heart attack, I would surely die of a broken heart. I didn't know any of this as I sped through the tunnel. I just knew that something somewhere had gone terribly wrong. If I wasn't at the dentist's getting my cavity filled, and I wasn't in the car with my mom driving home, then where was I? Did my mother even know where I was? Had anyone gotten permission from her for me to be in this tunnel? Maybe, I thought, she gave her permission as long as I would be back home in time for Thanksgiving. After all, we were going to be having a lot of people over to our house to celebrate the holiday. Surely my mom wouldn't want me to miss out on that. My mother was the major authority in our family— much more than my father, who hadn't wanted children in the first place. He used to tell my brothers and me, when he got mad at us, that we weren't even supposed to have been born. My mother's word was law. But as I flew through that tunnel heading I didn't know where, I realized I was dealing with a force even stronger, and that my mother couldn't get me out of this even if I wanted her to. *Maybe I won't have to go to school tomorrow,* I thought. I had to admit that missing school did rather appeal to me, as I knew I still had a ton of homework to do when I got home from the dentist!

I was starting to enjoy the ride — it was an incredible sensation, almost like being on a roller coaster at Adventureland — and not really feeling afraid, just anticipating what was to come. I knew this tunnel was going to lead me out to somewhere. The question was, where and when? I think on a subconscious level I knew I had died. I believe I was aware that my body was still back in that dentist's chair. The thing is that instead of feeling dead, my spirit had never felt more alive! I was brought up to believe that when you die, it's like going to sleep, and you don't feel a thing anymore. But, that was not turning out to be the case at all. Here I was dead — at least my body had died — and my soul had taken on a new life of its own. In fact, I felt almost proud of myself that my soul seemed to be handling things so well.

People talk about the light at the end of the tunnel, and all of a sudden that's exactly what I saw. The long speeding ride was over and I came out of the tunnel into the brightest light I'd ever seen. If you took a lampshade off a lamp and stared at the bare bulb for a long time, it would hurt your eyes. This was that same kind of blinding light, only many times brighter, and it didn't hurt at all. It was a magnificent, illuminating light that seemed to envelop me in its glory. It felt like I was being bathed in this light, almost purified. This was definitely not New York City! Nothing in my short fourteen years of life could have prepared me for the amazing vision of light I was seeing and the love that poured out along with it. A feeling of complete and utter love washed over me as I stood there. I was eager to learn more about what was happening and where I was — but the truth is that my soul knew even without being told. I knew my soul was entering a place where there was only pure and unconditional love, and I was sure it was a place I had never been in this lifetime. And then I saw who was waiting for me in the light, and I knew without a doubt I was in heaven.

Chapter 3

At Heaven's Door

Three figures were floating toward me—beautiful beings in long white gowns, with blue eyes and porcelain skin and soft waves of long golden hair, as thick and wavy as mine. Though I was standing on what felt like solid ground, they floated above it, and I saw that on their backs they had delicate white wings. I had no doubt that I was looking at my very own guardian angels! Each of them came to me and embraced me with great tenderness. "We're happy to see you," they said, and their voices were sweet and gentle. "We have been expecting you." I noticed that they all looked very much alike—the same beautiful hair and eyes and the same fluid way of moving. Maybe they were identical triplet angels, I thought, you never know.

They confirmed what I already knew, that there had been an accident at the dentist's and I had died there. They told me that they had been sent to wait for me and welcome me, and they assured me that I was safe with them in heaven. I knew I could believe them, because I felt their warmth and love all around me. *Wow,* I said to myself, *when I woke up this morning I thought it was going to be an ordinary day.* And now here I was in heaven with the angels! My angels started leading me away from the place where I'd landed. In the distance I saw a large gate looming up. The pearly gates? It must be! "We will take good care of you here," they said, "if you choose to stay." *Wait a minute,* I thought. *I get a choice?* "Yes," one of the angels said, as if they could hear inside my mind. "If you want to go back to your life, you can. But if you stay here, you'll have greater happiness than you can imagine. If you go back, your life will be very hard." "Um, okay," I said. "Let me think about this for a minute."

If I stayed here, would my hair always look as good as theirs? That may seem like a trivial thing, but I had just gotten a really bad haircut back on earth, so the thought of no more bad hair days definitely appealed to me. But I knew this was no time to be worrying about my hair. No, the thing I really had to worry about was my mother. I knew how devastated she would be if I never came back to my life. She was unhappy in her marriage to my dad, probably heading for divorce, and I was her only daughter. I couldn't leave her alone.

"I think I have to go back," I said to the angels. "My mom really needs me." "She will be hurt," one of the angels replied, "but she'll recover in time. And you'll be so much happier here. If you go back, you'll have to go through something so painful that you won't think you can survive it. You will survive, because we'll be watching over you. But if you stay here with us, you won't have to go through it at all." "We wish we could stop it from happening," a second angel said. "But we can't. Everything is already written in the book." "What does that mean?" I asked. "What book?" Then they explained to me that every second of our lives is predestined, mapped out for us before we are even born, and once we're born, not one thing about it can be changed. That was why they wanted me to stay: they knew what my life would hold if I chose to go back to it, and they wanted to spare me. *Don't tell me I will have to go through an even more horrendous haircut,* I thought. I couldn't help it—being fourteen, it was hard for me to think of anything worse they might be referring to.

We had passed through the gate by now and were crossing a meadow where all kinds of flowers in all different colors were blowing in a gentle breeze. Ahead of us there was a wall that extended as far as I could see in either direction, and in the wall there was a white door. Just a plain door, like you might have in your house. The angels stopped me with a gentle touch. "If you pass through this door, there is no turning back," one of them said. "You will have to stay here." "You'll be amazed at what is behind the door—so much more of glorious heaven!" said another. "And we can't wait to introduce you to everyone who is on the other side of it."

At that point I started to panic a little bit. I'm a Pisces, known to be the most indecisive sign of the zodiac as well as the most spiritually inclined. How could I make such a huge decision so quickly? Part of me did want to stay in heaven with the angels, where they were promising me peace and love and absolute joy. But part of me knew I just couldn't put my mother through that kind of grief. The woman who had endured a torturous labor (as she loved to remind me) and given birth to me, who told me her world stood still when she first laid eyes on me, whom I vomited on day in and day out as a baby because I got carsick every time I went in the car—the woman who I knew would sacrifice her own life for me—how could I be selfish enough to leave her behind without so much as a "Thank you, I love you"?

How did this happen? I thought. *How did I go from getting a cavity filled at the dentist to choosing my fate at the door of heaven?* I thought choosing between Novocain and nitrous oxide was a pretty big decision—you can imagine my dilemma, being faced with the choice between life as I knew it and a life that would be so much greater. I wished that everyone on earth could know what I knew about heaven now! There were times I had asked my mother or my grandmother where people go when they die, and they would say, "To heaven." If I asked what heaven was like, they would say, "It's very peaceful." And if I asked what it felt like to be dead, they would say it was just like sleeping. They did not think there was anything more to it than that. Boy, were they wrong!

The angels gathered around me. "There's something we want to show you before you make your choice," they said. Suddenly it was like I was looking through a window into a room I'd never seen before. There were chairs in rows, and people milling around, and a lot of flowers arranged around a closed casket of dark wood at the front of the room. I realized with a shock that the angels were showing me my funeral— the way it would be if I decided to stay in heaven. *My* body was in that casket. I wondered what I was wearing in there and whether someone had fixed my hair so the bad haircut didn't look so bad. I was only fourteen years old. I had never been to any funeral, let alone my own!

And let me tell you, it was not a pretty sight. My mother was sitting close to the casket, racked with sobs that I could hear all the way up in heaven. As I watched her, she doubled over in her chair. "Elissa," I heard her pleading, and it tore at my heart. "Come back, don't leave me, please come back to me." My grandmother went to try and console her, but she just screamed louder. And let me tell you something, that woman has a loud and piercing voice. I felt a little sorry for my grandmother, being right there next to her. I thought, *It's a good thing Grandma is hard of hearing, or that voice would make the poor woman go deaf!*

My father stayed where he was, in a chair near the wall, looking sullen. I sensed that he was struggling with regret for the times he had treated me badly and told me he'd never wanted me, as if that could have had something to do with my death. The room was full of people—I saw my brothers, other family and friends, neighbors, even some of my teachers—but my eyes kept coming back to my mother in her agony.

"Please come back, baby," she cried, almost as if she knew I had the choice. "See?" I said to the angels. "She really needs me. I have to go back." "Think carefully," they said. My mother would get over her pain, they told me, but I would only get this one chance to stay in heaven—or I would have to live a whole challenging lifetime before I could get there again. I felt so torn it's almost impossible to describe. There were two places I felt I had to be, and I could only be in one. If only it were as easy as living six months of the year in New York and the other six months in Florida or California, like some people do—but this wasn't about being a snowbird, and bicoastal living wasn't an option!

Every time the angels promised me the light and love of heaven, I inched closer to the door in the wall, and every time I looked back at my mother, I inched away from it. I knew I had to make a decision somehow. "Your mother will be okay," the angels said again. "We know you love each other very much, but we must tell you that if you go back, your relationship won't be as good as you think it will." They said that my mother and I would always have a deep bond—we would always know what the other was thinking and be able to finish each other's sentences—but it would be a turbulent relationship too, and no bed of roses. Hearing that, and at the same time feeling the light and love around me in heaven that I knew would be just about impossible to find on earth, I felt I had made my decision. "Okay, I think I'll stay," I told the angels.

As the words were leaving my mouth, my mother flung herself onto the casket with a wail of pure anguish. All she was screaming now was my name. I started to cry. I felt so helpless. I said to the angels as they put their comforting arms around me, "I don't know what to do!" Then suddenly the angels stepped back a little. I heard footsteps coming from somewhere. I knew it wasn't another angel, because these angels seemed to float, not walk. I heard a new voice, deep and strong.

"What's the matter, my child?" the voice said. "Why are you so upset? Why are you crying?" And I turned around—and God was standing there.

Chapter 4

Meeting God in Heaven

Through the mist of my tears, I could not believe my eyes: I was standing in the very presence of God. I guess we really are created in God's image, because he appeared in human form, tall and imposing. What struck me the most was how He looked so much like the pictures you see of Jesus Christ, only older. Not too much older, just a little—I don't want to insult God! It did make perfect sense, I realized, being that Jesus is said to be the son of God. Still, it was amazing to see that God and Jesus looked that much alike. I suppose that's why my daughter looks just like me, as Jesus looks like his father!

God was dressed in a long white robe with gold embroidering on it and a rope belt of braided gold with tousled fringes. He had on brown leather gladiator sandals and He walked with a cane that was embellished with gold. His hair was a rich brown color, long and a little wavy. His eyes were a beautiful shade of brown, full of warmth and expression, with a depth to them that exceeded oceans and oceans of time, distance, and dimension. I had always wanted blue eyes, but now I was so glad to see that God's eyes were a similar color to mine. I thought to myself, *God could have chosen to have any eye color that He wanted, and He did not choose blue.* In that instant, I embraced my brown eyes, and never wished for blue eyes again!

How can I possibly put into words what it felt like to be standing in the glory of God? My God, everyone's God! People spend their whole lives searching for God, wondering who or what God is, or whether God exists at all—and here I was face to face with Him. My tears dried up as if God had wiped them away from me Himself. *I should be making mental notes,* I thought, *because everybody's going to want to know what God looks like.* But standing in His powerful presence, I was too overwhelmed to think clearly. I couldn't even speak. I opened my mouth to utter something—perhaps a "Pleased to meet you" or "Hello, God, it's you!"—but as hard as I tried, I could not get a single word out of my mouth. It was as if someone had turned the volume down to zero in my voice box, because my mouth was open, but no sound was coming out. *This is a miracle,* I remember saying to myself. In truth, this sort of thing happening to me was beyond miraculous.

By this time my lovely guardian angels had moved back a bit to clear the way for my little—or shall I say huge, extraordinary—meeting with God. They seemed to want to give God and me a little bit of privacy, because they lingered lovingly in the background while we stood face to face with each other. Still I could not speak; I was as starstruck as I'd always thought I would be if I met John Stamos or Rob Lowe. Although I must say this was a million times stronger than, say, how impressed you might feel if you met your favorite movie star. I knew it was much more of an honor to be face to face with God, my heavenly father and the creator of the universe! I glanced over at my guardian angels, as if needing their reassurance to let me know that this was really happening. They smiled at me and nodded their heads to let me know that yes, indeed, I was with God. Once again, I tried to get a word out, but again nothing. God must have had enough of my teenage admiration. To my relief, He took the liberty of speaking to me first.

"What's the matter, my child?" He asked. "Why are you so upset? Why are you crying?" When He called me His child, I felt a wash of love from Him more powerful than anything I'd ever experienced. In that very moment, I knew that God was my one and only father in heaven. It didn't matter to me anymore that I had such an unloving dad on earth, a dad who didn't even want me. I knew that God was my father here. It started to make perfect sense to me why some of my friends had the most caring dads and I did not—something that used to make me jealous sometimes as I wondered why my own father couldn't show me he cared. The reason, I told myself, was that God knew I would meet Him in heaven, and no other person in the world would get to do that but me. It was worth having a lousy dad on earth to see, hear, and feel all of God's light and love pour through me in heaven, as it was doing now.

I knew God was waiting for a reply. Finally words came out of my mouth, the volume turned back up in my voice box. I said in a panicky voice, "I have to go back to my mother. She really needs me." That was all I had to say to Him, because He told me He understood. His tone of voice was strong and powerful, yet protective and loving at the same time, and I sensed that he could see the truth behind my words. He knew that even though I'd said I needed to go back, I was still uncertain of what I really wanted to do. There was nothing I would have loved to do more than to stay in heaven with Him and my guardian angels, where there is nothing but pure, unconditional light and love. I was basking in it—in all His glory, the splendor and magnificent love that you can only truly know and feel when you are standing before God in heaven. All of a sudden the calmest feeling washed over me, and I was totally at peace knowing that I had just surrendered my indecision to God. It was in His hands now, and He would find the right answer. I knew He would make the best decision for me, as nobody knew me or my soul better than He did!

With that, God turned to the angels and said, "Send her back immediately!" Then He turned back to me. "I am sending you back with a very important purpose," He told me. I was being sent back as His messenger, to do some of His work in heaven here on earth. I was being asked to educate people all over the world about God's light and love.

Now my guardian angels were hovering around us in a semicircle. They said to me, "Once you return to your life, you will not remember for many years what you were just told." They said that it would simply be too overwhelming for me now—much too much of a responsibility at such a young age. And I did have to admit that being sent back from heaven as God's messenger might be a little bit—okay, a lot—earth-shattering for a teenager to handle! I agreed that it would be too much of a responsibility at only fourteen years old. I thought it might be nice to grow up, graduate high school, go to college, fall in love, get married, and have kids before I changed the world! Knowing that I was God's messenger on earth was serious business. I just wanted to go back to being that carefree, goofy teenager who was happy to be voted the funniest in school. Being God's messenger and an angel on earth would all come in due time. I told God that I accepted my fate, and He did show me one more thing before I left heaven, a glimpse of what my life would be like in years to come. More on that later!

My guardian angels gave me a warm goodbye embrace, and God did too. "Thank you," I said to them all. "I hope you're not mad at me for not choosing to stay in heaven with you." The angels sweetly laughed and said, "Of course not—you're being sent back with a very important purpose. We will be watching over you always, and when you're ready to come back here, we will be waiting for you in the light again." Then they told me that I would not be coming back to heaven for a very long time, that I was going to live a long life doing God's work on earth. I thought to myself, *What a lucky girl I am! What could be better than that?* God smiled at me and said, "Remember, once your soul is back in your body and you return to your life, you will not remember your purpose for being sent back until the time is right." "I understand," I said. Then I watched as God walked back to His throne and sat down in His great king's chair, where He continued to watch over the world.

Chapter 5

The Return

Once again I was back in the speeding tunnel, only this time I knew exactly where it was going to lead me: back to my body and the life I knew before the dentist killed me. To say that I had mixed emotions would be putting it mildly. Here I was, a fourteen-year-old girl with her whole life ahead of her, who had it taken from her in the blink of an eye, only to have it given back just as quickly! The saying "Life is just a moment of eternity" certainly comes to mind. You know how when you're traveling in a car or on a train or plane, it always seems to take forever to get where you're going, then it feels so much quicker on the way home? While my soul was traveling through the speeding tunnel on the return trip to my body, it seemed much faster than the trip to heaven. Before I knew it, I had come to the tunnel's end. Just as my soul was about to enter my body again, I heard the dentist screaming, "Don't give up! Keep trying—we have to get her back!" I felt the hygienist doing CPR on me, quick hard thrusts to my chest, and blowing air into my mouth. "There's still no pulse," she gasped. "Oh, God," the dentist moaned. "We can't lose her. We have to bring her back." The hygienist did another round of compressions. I was back in my body now, and I wanted to yell, "Hey, could you take it easy on my chest?" That was the first pain I'd felt in the whole experience—there was no pain when I left my body and certainly no pain in heaven— and I must have had enough of it, because all of a sudden the hygienist cried, "We have a pulse now! She's back!" I opened my eyes and saw the same bare walls of the examining room— still no diplomas on the walls, and now I had a pretty good idea why. "Thank God," I heard the dentist say, and I laughed to myself. *If you only knew.* He had no idea that I'd already thanked

God myself, in person.

"What happened?" I said to the dentist, a little dazed and confused. "You had too much nitrous," he blurted out. He must have been too relieved to think about liability, otherwise he might not have been in such a hurry to admit it! "I was just in heaven," I said. I was starting to feel a little bit queasy and very, very tired. "I bet you were," he said. He was almost in tears. "I believe it, because you were gone. You *died*." He told me that they'd almost given up and called 911, but because I was only a teenager, he kept telling the hygienist not to stop trying. I felt like telling him it wasn't the CPR that brought me back, it was God himself who'd made the final decision to let me return to my life. But as groggy as I was, I didn't feel like getting into such a deep conversation with the man who'd just killed me. Still, I couldn't help but feel compassion for him when I saw how shaken up he really was. In fact, he seemed to need more comforting than I did! I suppose my experience had already changed me, because I seemed to be a more compassionate person all of a sudden. "It's okay," I told him. "I understand. It was an accident."

"Do you forgive me?" he asked, and I told him I did. For his sake, I was glad that I had chosen to come back, because I don't think he could have handled the guilt he would have felt had I not returned to my life. Perhaps he had children of his own, and the thought of killing someone else's child might have been more than he could bear. I asked him where my mother was, and he said she was still in the waiting room, without a clue as to what had just happened. "Let's not upset her," he said. "I'll just tell her you had a bad reaction to the nitrous oxide and I couldn't finish filling the cavity." And that was exactly what he told her, adding, "I think she should go home and take it easy for the rest of the day." What he failed to mention was that I needed to go home and rest up from being dead! I'm certain that if she had known that, she would have rushed me to the emergency room for observation to make sure I didn't stop breathing again. Years later, I heard on the news that a seventeen-year-old girl died the same way I did, at the dentist, after receiving too much nitrous oxide. My next-door neighbor's dentist killed himself the same way. I wonder if I'm the only person who lived to tell? As my mother and I walked out of the clinic, she looked at me, puzzled. "What went on in there?" she asked me. But I was afraid to tell her the whole story, afraid that somehow she'd say it was my fault, since teenagers always seem to get a bum rap! So I chose to keep it to myself for a while, and I just shrugged off her question. All I said was, "Don't ever take me there again." "Don't worry, I won't," she said. It was the most surreal feeling to go from life to heaven and then back again, all so fast. This was the stuff that movies were made of—yet this was real life! I could hardly believe I was here, in the middle of the Times Square shopping center, when just minutes ago I'd been standing in a field of flowers in front of heaven's gate.

I followed my mother next door to the supermarket to do our Thanksgiving meal shopping, and I walked around bewildered with her, pushing the cart through the aisles in a daze while she filled it with stuffing mix and sweet potatoes and cranberries. Nothing around me seemed real anymore. Part of me already missed heaven and all the glory of it. Meeting God was the most incredible thing that had ever happened to me, and I just wasn't ready to share that with my mother yet. But I did share it with my best friend.

After we got home that day, I went with Amy to get her hair cut, and while she was waiting for the stylist, I told her everything: about the dentist giving me too much gas, cutting off my oxygen supply, and killing me. I told her how my soul was in heaven, and met my guardian angels, and met God. I told her you should never be afraid to die, because heaven was the most beautiful place you could be in. "Wow," Amy said. "That is so wild!" typical teenager talk. But I could tell my story had made an impression on her, though. She told me I must be really special to meet God and have Him let me come back to my life. Then she thanked me for telling her how beautiful heaven was. She said, "Now I won't be afraid to die." It made me feel good to hear her say that I was special, but I made her promise not to tell anyone at school, because I didn't want anyone to look at me differently. As it was, there were some girls who were jealous of me because they knew I was a model. Can you imagine if they knew I was chosen by God to meet Him in heaven? So I made Amy do a pinky swear with me that she would keep it to herself, and as far as I know, she did. The next day in school, when my teacher asked me where my homework was, I said, "Would you believe that my dog ate it?" Not surprisingly, she said no. I thought to myself, *Then you definitely won't believe that I died, went to heaven, had a meeting with God, and didn't have time to do it!*

As I'd vowed when I was in the tunnel, I did make it back home to my mother for Thanksgiving, and what a joyous holiday it was for me. No one knew more than I how that day could have been anything but a celebration if I'd stayed in heaven. Instead of enjoying a Thanksgiving feast, my family would have been mourning me at my funeral. Seeing the joy on my mother's face that day confirmed to me over and over again how right I'd been to come back for her, my sweet, gentle, loving mother. The woman who dedicated her life to me in so many countless ways. It didn't matter that she didn't yet know the whole story of what had happened to me; I knew that this was the greatest gift I could have given her. That Thanksgiving will always be my favorite, my most memorable one. I'll never forget being gathered around the table with my whole family, with my beloved grandma, Lily, at the head, telling jokes to one another as we ate, watching her eyes light up with laughter. She truly did have a smile that could light up any room. And on that day, not only did her smile light up the room, I truly felt

God's light all around us. As my mom piled another helping of turkey on my plate, one I knew I would soon be slipping to my wonderful German shorthaired pointer Shag who lay patiently under the table waiting for it, I silently said a prayer to God, thanking Him for giving me the precious gift of life and a very important purpose in it—one I knew would be revealed to me when the time was right.

Chapter 6

Transformed by the Light

How does a teenager die one day, go to heaven, meet her guardian angels, have a one-on-one conference with God, get appointed his messenger on earth, and still remain the same person? She doesn't! I may have looked the same physically, but mentally and emotionally I was not the same fourteen-year-old I was before I entered that tunnel. I knew I was different somehow; I came back from heaven a spiritual being, transformed by the light that had enveloped me there. God had told me that I wouldn't remember my reason for being sent back until years later, and that was true. I remembered everything else that had taken place. I remembered the long speeding tunnel that had transported my soul to heaven. I remembered my three beautiful guardian angels waiting for me in the light to let me know that I was safe with them there. I remembered God walking over to me, asking, "What's the matter, my child? Why are you so upset? Why are you crying?" And I remembered the tremendous outpouring of light and love that I felt in His presence, so powerful that I never wanted to leave. But I didn't remember why He had sent me back to my life. I just knew it was supposed to be revealed to me when the time was right—and I didn't know when that was going to be.

Day after day, I would try to make sense of it, thinking to myself, *Why did God choose me out of everyone else?* It must have been for a reason. In my short life, I knew that this sort of thing just didn't happen to other people. I knew that people died and went to heaven, but how many of them were sent back to earth with a special purpose as part of God's plan? How had I come to be God's chosen one? All I could think of was that I was a very gentle, loving, compassionate soul—the kind of girl who took in every stray dog on the street. I fed all the stray cats in my neighborhood and never missed a day; I was out there taking care of them even in blizzards. Even injured birds would find their way to my doorstep, as if they somehow knew I would take care of them too.

My mother always thought it was because I was a Pisces, which is supposed to be the kindest sign of the zodiac, as well as the most spiritual (not to mention the most indecisive, as I discovered in heaven when I had to choose to stay or leave!). "My daughter is such a sensitive girl," she would say. Once, when I was about nine, she took me to the pet store in the Times Square shopping center. I couldn't bear to see the dogs cooped up in those small cages, so when no one was looking, I opened them all up and let all the dogs out. I thought I was doing a good deed, and so did they! The manager of the pet store didn't see it that way, of course, and after he'd rounded up the dogs and put them all back in their cages, I got a good lecture from him that I was never, ever, under any circumstances to do that again. I obediently said I understood, all the while secretly glad those dogs had had a moment of joy.

I had been that way before my near-death experience, but after I came back from heaven, I was even more so. Now I couldn't bear the thought of suffering in the world; I felt everyone else's pain, people and animals alike, as if it were my own. I wished I could take it away so that I would hurt, not them. That may be an unusual thing for a fourteen-year-old to feel, as most teenagers—most people, in fact—are pretty self-centered and tend to put their own needs ahead of others. But I honestly would have given my life if it would help spare others suffering, if it would save other lives. Perhaps that was why I did die, to do just that: help save lives.

As the weeks and months went on after my return, I didn't remember my purpose—that wouldn't come for many years—

but I did start to have flashbacks of my near-death experience and my time spent in heaven. They came at me fast and without warning. I could be sitting in class at school, or walking through the park with my friends, and all of a sudden it would feel like a jolt of electricity hit me—just the way I imagined it would feel to be struck by lightning. All the sensations of my time in heaven would come flooding back, every second of it running through me with such force that it would stop me in my tracks and I'd hold my head in my hands until it stopped. "Are you all right?" my friends would ask, because it must have looked like I was in pain. I wasn't, but the sensation was so powerful that I couldn't move. I took it as a sign that God and my guardian angels were letting me know they were with me, watching over me. I had many nights when I missed heaven so much I couldn't sleep. In my mind, I felt that these flashbacks were God's way of letting me know that I was still close to Him, and that heaven wasn't too far away.

I wondered if other people could sense the change in me, and some of the time I believed they did. One friend told me, "You're different from any other person I have ever met." Then, the summer before I entered tenth grade, my parents had our house appraised, as they were thinking of selling it and wanted to see what they could get. The appraiser brought a friend with her, who just happened to be an evangelist. After he walked into my room and introduced himself to me, he turned to my mother and said, "Your daughter is very special." "I know," my mother said. What mother wouldn't agree with someone who says her child is special?

"She is special for a reason," he insisted. "She is an angel." I thought to myself, *Different, special, angel, that's great—but could somebody please tell me what the reason was?*

It didn't matter how much I wondered or worried, I wouldn't know that until God was ready for me to know it. But I did notice another way I was different when I started to feel more and more protective of my mother. After all, she was the reason I'd felt I had to come back. I knew she was in an unhappy marriage to my father, and I felt she really needed me. She would always tell me how blessed she was with me, that I was the sunshine in her life. And there were many times since coming back from heaven when I'd choose to spend the day with her instead of hanging out at the mall with my friends. So many of them were constantly arguing with *their* moms—not me. My mother and I hardly ever fought. As I've said, my dad had never wanted children, and I didn't have much of a relationship with him, so my mother was basically all I had, and I always tried to make her happy. Since we both had a good sense of humor—we'd both been voted the funniest in school—I always knew how to put a smile on her face. In some ways, I felt like I was her mother instead of the other way around, and I'm sure she would agree with that too, as I was always the one she turned to for advice. "You're wise beyond your years," she would say to me. I preferred to think of it as being transformed by the light!

My mother, in fact, was becoming my best friend, the person I felt I could confide in most. That was why I did finally decide to tell her about my near-death experience. While I didn't tell her every detail—I left out the part about the difficult life ahead of me, and I didn't mention the glimpse I'd had of my funeral—I did tell her that my soul went to heaven while the dentist was giving me CPR. She was fascinated, but she never pushed me to reveal more of it to her until I was ready.

The angels had said that everything was written in the book. They had also told me that I would never be perfectly happy here on earth, because I'd always be wishing I could get back to heaven, although that would not happen for a long time. And, indeed, I sometimes thought longingly about heaven and the perfect love I'd felt there. *When you're lonely*, the angels had told me, *you'll feel something stroking your hair, and you'll know we are there to comfort you.* Every once in a while I did imagine that I felt that light, loving touch, and it always brought me peace. Then the angels sent me something even better.

Chapter 7

A Match Made in Heaven

I woke up that November morning realizing it was my one-year anniversary, exactly one year to the day since I had my near-death experience. With a stretch and a yawn, I hopped out of bed figuring the same thing I had thought one year earlier: that today was going to be no different from any other ordinary day. I couldn't have been more wrong. Little did I know that today my lovely guardian angels were busy in heaven, about to play Cupid on me.

One thing I knew was going to be different. After school, Amy and I had tickets to go to a concert called Soaps Alive, where a full roster of our favorite soap-opera stars would appear in person on stage. We were so excited, because we knew that John Stamos, who just happened to be the hottest teenage heartthrob on the #1 soap, *General Hospital*, would be there, along with the rest of the *General Hospital* cast. Even for a girl who had already died and gone to heaven, not many things were more exciting than the prospect of meeting John Stamos!

"Maybe we can sneak backstage and meet him after the show," I said to Amy on the way to school. "Like, how are we supposed to do that?" Then she thought about it for a second. "Knowing you, you'll find a way!" She knew that when I was determined to do something, practically nothing could stand in my way. So we made a plan that when security wasn't looking, we would make a run for it, straight into John's dressing room. "If we don't get arrested, it just might work," I said.

As it turned out, our plan was never executed, because we got picked at the door to go backstage and meet the whole cast after the show. Coincidence? Absolutely not! Everything always happens for a reason. Amy chalked it up to a stroke of good luck, while I knew that every second of our lives is already written in the book, and there are no coincidences. This was definitely part of the angels' plan.

We sat through the whole two-hour show, just waiting to get backstage. Not that the show wasn't good! My favorite part was when John played drums with a local rock band. I couldn't help noticing the adorable bass guitar player, and as I watched John, my eyes kept going back to him. "Isn't he cute?" I said to Amy. "Yeah, John is gorgeous," she said. "Not John," I said. "The bass player. " "Who did you come to see, some bass player or John Stamos?" Amy had on a cut-off T-shirt that said "I Love John" in big letters. I was wearing one just like it. I had to admit she was right.

When the show finally ended, Amy and I couldn't have run any faster. We flashed security our backstage passes, then ran through the doors, and I ran straight into John Stamos! I wasn't sure if it was because I was wearing an "I Love John" shirt or because he liked the way I looked, but he actually started to flirt with me. He asked me if I was an actress. I said I was only a model. "With your looks, you could be an actress," he said. John's manager was with him, and he handed me his card, telling me to call him when I graduated. I shoved his card in the pocket of my skin-tight jeans. To this day I wonder why I never took him up on his offer. Probably because I knew I would make a lousy actress!

Anyway, there we were, talking and flirting with the hottest soap star on the scene, when I spotted that handsome bass guitar player standing behind John, staring at me. Now, don't get me wrong; John was a very good-looking guy, every schoolgirl's fantasy (not to mention some of their mothers' too). But there was just something about that bass player. While John was in the middle of a sentence, the lead singer of the band walked by, and I interrupted John to ask him, "Who is that?" "That's Ron," the singer said. "He plays bass in my band. You want to meet him? Come on, I'll introduce you." I thought to myself, *Goodbye John, hello Ron!* John looked a little amused, as I'm sure he wasn't used to being tossed aside for another guy. Sorry, John, but for me it was love at first sight.

Hank, the singer, led me over to him, and as he introduced us, I literally felt my knees go weak. Ron was the classic tall-dark-and-handsome, with these big, brown puppy-dog eyes, a cleft in his chin, and the cutest crooked smile. Sweetest of all, he was actually pretty shy with me. I was just thrilled that he seemed as interested in me as I was in him. You'd think he would have been full of himself, being so good-looking and playing in a rock band, but he wasn't. He was just a really nice, cool guy. Almost hesitantly, he asked if he could drive me home. *Well, twist my arm!* Of course I said yes. I'd forgotten all about poor Amy!

Ron and I went out for a burger and fries and got to know each other a little. I learned that he was seventeen, a senior in high school; I was just fifteen and a sophomore. He said he loved playing bass in his band more than anything. I told him everything about myself, well, almost everything: I didn't tell him that a year ago to the day I had died, gone to heaven, and met God. I figured that could wait until our second date! When he finally did drive me home, he parked in front of my house and we shared the sweetest kiss. He gave me some Polaroids from the concert, showing him in the band, with John Stamos on drums, and I gave him a slide from one of my modeling sessions. He put it in his guitar case and said he would keep it there forever. That night before I went to sleep, I thanked God and my angels for playing Cupid with me and Ron. I knew this could only be a match made in heaven — an anniversary present from my angels and God.

The next day at school I took the J and the H off my "I Love John" shirt and replaced the J with an R. Now it said, "I Love Ron"! A friend of mine came up to me and said, "Elissa, you're glowing!" "I'm in love," I explained. And for the first time since I came back from heaven, I was truly happy. Being with Ron felt as close to heaven as I could get here on earth. He was my saving grace—and my first true love.

For the rest of that school year we hung out whenever we could, made out whenever we got the chance; I lost my virginity to him in the back seat of his gold Firebird when I was just sweet sixteen. We were quite a pair, the cool rock star and the hot model; we were like two peas in a pod. And I was so happy in love that I could put heaven on hold for a little while and just live my life here on earth. But, as they say, all good things must come to an end. With Ron being two years older than me, he went off to college, and even though we promised to keep in touch, I knew it wouldn't be the same. As crushed as I was, I told myself the old saying: *If you love something, set it free. If it comes back to you, it's yours. If it doesn't, it never was.*

In the meantime, I just happened to meet another bass guitar player who lived in the same town as Ron, Valley Stream. A coincidence? Absolutely not. Remember, there are no coincidences! His name was Greg Smith, and today he is bass guitar player for Ted Nugent. But, at the time he was in a fairly well-known band called the Plasmatics, with Wendy O. Williams as lead singer, and a pretty wild one at that—at least she appeared that way on stage. Off stage she was the nicest person you could ever meet, and straight-laced too; she didn't drink or do any drugs. Anyway, I was seventeen and Greg was twenty-four, and at that age I thought he was really an older man. We hung out whenever he was in town, but a lot of the time he was off touring with Wendy and the Plasmatics.

And as cool as Greg was, deep down, if truth be told, my heart still belonged to Ron. I kept telling myself, *If you love something, set it free. If it comes back to you, it's yours.* And... he came back for one sweet, passionate night. I was nineteen and he was twenty-one. We went to dinner, to the movies, and then to bed. It was all so bittersweet, because I didn't know if we were picking up where we left off or if we'd go our separate ways again. And we did go our separate ways: Ron returned to college, and I resumed my modeling career.

Around this time there was a second Soaps Alive concert. This time I went with another friend, who happened to be good friends with John Stamos, so I didn't have to worry about sneaking backstage or getting picked at the door; my friend already had backstage passes. I felt a little sad knowing that Ron was away at school and his band wouldn't be there this time. As I walked backstage after the show, I had my back to a roped-off staircase when an eager fan pushed me hard trying to get to John. I fell backwards, head over heels, over the rope, and did backflips all the way down those steep metal stairs. John saw the whole thing and yelled for someone to call 911 as he ran down the steps after me. "Don't move," he said. "An ambulance is on its way." "I don't need an ambulance," I told him. All I had were some cuts and bruises and, as it turned out, a sprained ankle. John scooped me up gently in his arms and carried me back up the steep steps. When he looked in my face, he broke out in a big grin. "Wait a second," he laughed. "I know you. Aren't you the girl from the other Soaps Alive show? The one who dumped me for that bass player?" I laughed too. "Yes," I said. "But this time I fell head over heels for you, literally!" Once again, though, I had to admit that my heart still belonged to Ron. And once again I told myself: *If you love something, set it free...*

Part II

God's Messenger

Chapter 8

Visions and Signs

I knew from the start that heaven had changed me. It hadn't just given me a new way of thinking about the world, it had given me a new way of *seeing*. Just a few months after I died and came back, in the summer before I was going into tenth grade, I had a dream that I was at a fair with my best friend, Amy. We were having fun walking around the booths and games when all of a sudden a good-looking guy walked over and started talking to me. "I'm Adam," he said. In the dream I was very attracted to this boy named Adam, so when he asked me for my phone number, I gladly gave it to him! I woke up the next morning to a warm, bright summer day, happy as always to be out of school. Just as I was about to climb out of bed, the phone on my bedside table rang. All the girls in my school wanted their own private phone lines, and I felt lucky to actually have one! I picked up and it was Amy, calling to see if I wanted to go with her later that day to a fair they were having at St. Anthony's Church in town. "Sure, that sounds like fun," I said. "I'll see you later." I didn't even think of my dream. But at the fair later on, Amy and I were playing the ring toss, trying to win one of the big stuffed animals hanging on the back wall, when I noticed a good-looking guy standing nearby watching us. When I caught his eye, he stepped forward. "Hi," he said. "I'm Adam." I screamed! "Oh my God," I said, "it's *you*! You're the same guy I met in my dream last night!" It really was him—he looked exactly the same—and I couldn't help wondering if I was losing my mind. He looked at me as if I actually might be a little crazy, or as if he couldn't be sure if I was kidding around with him or not. But I kept saying over and over again, "I'm psychic. I must be psychic! I had a dream of you last night, that I met you today, and here you are!" Fortunately, he believed me and didn't take off running! Sure enough, he asked me for my phone number and told me he would call me the next day. Which he did, and I found out he was fifteen like me and had just moved to Oceanside. We hung out all summer, and though I wasn't in love with him, I did like him a lot. To this day, I still refer to him as my dream guy!

I'm not sure I would have connected my prophetic boyfriend dream with my trip to heaven if it hadn't been for a story my beloved grandmother Lily told me. She was in her thirties when she had to have an abortion for medical reasons. In those days it wasn't as safe as it is now, and something went wrong. She bled so severely that she lost consciousness, and the doctor couldn't get a pulse. While he was trying, my grandmother said, she found herself speeding through a long tunnel. I'm sure it was the same one I was in! There must be only one way into heaven, and that's it. Anyway, she reached there, and who was waiting for her in the light but her own grandfather. She was so happy to see him, and she reached out her hand to him, but he wouldn't take it. He told her it was not her time to be in heaven yet and she must go back. Then he disappeared. My grandmother went back through the tunnel and back into her body, just at the moment the doctor found a pulse—just the way I did. And she was changed too. One night she dreamed that her father passed away, and when her doorbell rang the next morning, when she opened it and saw her sister standing there, she said, "Don't tell me, I already know Poppy's dead."

When I heard that, the change in me made more sense. I think that people who have had a near-death experience do have this sixth sense, and I think they can always find each other. It's one reason why my grandmother and I shared such a strong spiritual connection and still do. Everyone who has had a near-death experience shares certain similarities: they talk about becoming one with an indescribable light, feeling a deep sense of connectedness with the totality of creation, a strong sense of belonging and gratitude, and a renewed sense of meaning and purpose.

Over the years some people who've had near-death experiences have surprised me by finding me! One day when I was shopping at Whole Foods with my daughter, a woman who worked there came up to us and said, "I know you and your daughter are very special. You are psychic, and so is your daughter, but she is too young to understand it yet." "Well, you must be psychic yourself," I said, "because you're absolutely right. I'm psychic because I had a near-death experience." I left out the part about being sent back as God's messenger; I don't just tell that to everyone I meet! "You're kidding," she said. "So did I." And then she told me about two experiences, one when she was just a baby and had double pneumonia, the other as a grown woman when she was in a bad car accident. "Did you go to heaven?" I asked her. And she said she had gone through a tunnel—yes, that tunnel!—and into the light, but all she saw of heaven was a beautiful garden, with the most exquisitely-colored flowers she had ever seen.

Over the years, after that first dream of Adam, I continued to have dreams that came true. Sometimes it took amusing forms, like the time I dreamed that I was teaching an aerobics class—I actually was an aerobics instructor at the time—and I broke the nail on my right pinky. The next day I was teaching a class when my pinky nail broke off! I had long nails, so it wasn't easy to miss; it was on the floor right next to me. I picked it up and showed it to everyone in the class. "Would you believe I had a dream about this last night?" I asked. "That this exact nail fell off my finger?" Everyone sort of gasped, I laughed, and said that I wished I would dream the winning lottery numbers!

Other times I dreamed about more serious things. I dreamed that my niece Adina was away at sleepaway camp and got hurt at the swimming pool, and it turned out that she had, though thankfully she was all right. And sometimes my signs didn't come in dreams at all. One day at 3:55pm—I noticed the time—I suddenly, and for no reason I could tell, went to my computer, googled Whitney Houston, and started reading all about her life. It made no sense, since I wasn't a big fan of hers, even though I thought she was a gifted singer; the Bee Gees were more my taste! Later that evening, when I was watching TV, the news broke in announcing that Whitney Houston had died earlier that day. She had been pronounced dead at exactly 3:55pm. Then, a couple of years ago, I walked into my kitchen and suddenly said out loud, "Oh God, Brad has cancer!" Brad, my eldest brother (and Adina's father), was only forty-six at the time. I got upset with myself for saying such a terrible thing—until the phone rang later that night and it was Brad, calling with news from the doctor that he had thyroid cancer. Fortunately, his cancer was caught early and it was treatable, and today Brad is cancer-free. You can imagine that Brad's family is always asking me if I've had any more dreams or premonitions about them. I always reply, "If I do, I'll let you know!"

Once I went to a noted psychic to get a reading, and she laughed at me. "What are you doing here?" she said. "You know, you're psychic yourself." "I know," I said, "but even the best chef likes to eat in someone else's restaurant sometimes!"

I've always heard that birds are messengers of spirit; they will come to you to deliver a message and warn you when you're about to lose a loved one. It makes perfect sense, since a bird's spirit flies so free and soars so high. I always say that in my next lifetime, I want to come back as a bird so I can fly that free and not be held back by anyone or anything. So that if I'm not happy, I can just pick up and fly away to a better place. I remember well one time when a bird brought me a sign I wished I hadn't seen. First I have to back up and start by saying that I mentioned earlier when I was growing up, we had a wonderful German shorthaired pointer named Shag. I never knew why my dad named him that when he was smooth-coated and short-haired; the name Shag belongs on a scruffy long-haired dog, if you ask me! Whatever the case, Shag was a very special dog, and when he died, I knew how much my mom missed him, so a couple of years later I surprised her with another one.

This German shorthaired pointer was the runt of the litter, a tiny puppy with big paws and spots all over him, and I thought he was rather adorable. Unfortunately, his littermates didn't see him that way, as they were all ganging up on him, and instead of trying to defend himself, all he did was cry. I told the breeder, "I'll take him, but let's hope he toughens up a little bit."

Well, he never did. This dog—my mom named him Cody— was afraid of his own shadow. He would run the other way if he saw a Chihuahua coming! The funny thing is, you'd never have known he was the runt of the litter, because he grew to be the largest German shorthaired pointer I'd ever seen. His paws were as big as a Great Dane's. My mom called him a gentle giant. He lived to fourteen years old, and the day he died, before I knew about it, I was driving home after dropping my daughter off at preschool when out of the blue a big, beautiful seagull crashed into my windshield. I was so startled that at first I thought it had gone *through* the windshield, that's what a huge impact it made. Upon inspection, the windshield was all right, but the seagull wasn't. The poor injured bird was lying at the side of the road. I immediately called wildlife control, who came, only to tell me that the seagull was dead. "Can't you do CPR on it?" I cried. "Lady," they said, "we don't do CPR on birds!" I didn't have the heart to watch them dispose of the bird, so I sadly drove away. Even though I knew it wasn't my fault that the seagull flew into my windshield, I still felt awful about it. Little did I know that it was actually a sign from Cody. When I got home, my mom called me, crying, to tell me that he had died that day of a heart attack. When I asked her what time, it was the same time the seagull flew into my windshield and died. I knew it was a sign, which comforted both me and my mom. An even more comforting sign came the following morning. As I was getting out of bed, I looked out my window and saw something falling from the sky, landing on my window ledge. *Oh no,* I thought, *not another seagull!* But when I went to the window, to my amazement I saw the most beautiful starfish sitting on the ledge. I couldn't believe that after it fell from the sky and crashed on my window ledge, it was still in one piece. In fact, it was perfect. I thought to myself, *Where did this come from?* Then I smiled and realized that it was a sign—a beautiful sign from Cody *and* the seagull that they were alive and well in heaven. That perfect starfish stayed on my windowsill for one week. I assumed a seagull had dropped it from the sky—maybe the very same seagull that hit my windshield! My daughter would wake up every morning and run to look out the window at it. The morning it was gone, she said the starfish had needed to go cheer someone else up!

My mother was close to my dog too—an adorable miniature dachshund I named Frankie—and he even lived with her part of the time. You could say that we had joint custody of him! He was the sweetest, most adorable little fella you could ever hope to meet. This dog was loaded with personality; he could, and very often would, charm the pants off everyone he met! I lived at the time next door to Keyshawn Johnson, who was running back for the New York Jets then. Every time Keyshawn saw Frankie, he would laugh and say, "Man, that dog is full of charisma!" I was blessed with fourteen beautiful years with Frankie. Then one night I had a dream that Frankie died. In my dream, after that, I saw an image of Frankie's head on Shag's body, attached as one dog. I knew in my dream that they were both together in heaven. When I woke up the next morning, I knew right away that something was wrong with Frankie. He could hardly move, and I took him right to the vet. An X-ray showed that the dog had a huge mass in his stomach that had spread to his chest.

My beloved Frankie was full of cancer, and he had to be put to sleep that day. Ultimately, I didn't have the strength to watch Frankie being euthanized, so it was my mother who held him in her arms. She put her head down to kiss him goodbye, and Frankie, who used to shower my mother with kisses every day, was too weak to kiss her back. She whispered to him, "Can I have a kiss goodbye?" But he just couldn't lift his head, and he gently passed away in her arms.

The very next day she called me, her voice choked with emotion, and said, "Frankie came and kissed me goodbye!" She said that that night, when she was home from the vet's and sitting watching television, she suddenly had a vision of Frankie—and not just a vision: she actually felt a wet doggy kiss on her nose. He had come back to give her that kiss after all. Just before they put Frankie to sleep that day, I had a vision of my own, and it was amazing. I was crying my heart out when all of a sudden I saw God Himself. He was standing above me with His arms stretched out, just the way I had seen Him when I went to heaven, and He gently told me that it was time for Frankie to go back home to Him. He let me know that He was waiting for Frankie and would take good care of him in heaven. I stopped crying and smiled at God, nodding my head to show I understood, and thanking Him for blessing me with Frankie for fourteen beautiful years. As I sit here writing this now, tears come to my eyes all over again, but I cannot describe how comforting it was to know that God was waiting to welcome Frankie back into His glorious kingdom.

Chapter 9

The Angels' Warning

When I made my decision to return to life rather than stay in heaven, the angels warned me that a great challenge was in store for me — something so painful I wouldn't believe I could survive it. It wouldn't be long before I found out exactly what they meant. Up to that point, I don't think anyone ever accused me of being boy crazy, but truth be told, I probably was. My mom was always glad that I never got into drinking or drugs or any trouble with the law — but cute guys always did occupy my mind! I think I was constantly searching because my dad never gave me the love that I needed; I'd always been told that he never wanted kids, which made me feel so unloved. I know in my heart I searched for that love elsewhere. This time, it came in the arms of an older man — at least it seemed that way to me, as I was only nineteen years old and he was all of thirty-two! At the time I met him, I had no idea that he was a famous record producer and would go on to win five Grammys. His first was for Whitney Houston's album *I Want to Dance with Somebody*, the next was Madonna's *Vogue* — a huge hit in the '80s — and the list goes on. His name was Steve Thompson, and we met when a good friend of mine who had dated him briefly set us up. "I think you two will hit it off," she said. "He's a Scorpio." "Say no more," I said, as she knew I loved Scorpios, being a Pisces myself. I knew that Scorpio and Pisces are the best water-sign match in the zodiac, so if I wasn't quite interested yet, I was certainly intrigued!

We met at a nightclub called Zachary's, and I thought he was pretty cute, sexy in a rugged sort of way. And I could feel the chemistry between us — it must have been the Scorpio/ Pisces connection. He kept laughing at me, saying, "You are so adorable," and I kept laughing at him, thinking, *You are so hot!* What I liked about Steve was that he was mature, not like some of the boys I had known. This was a real man, and I was ready to have a real relationship with him. I dated him for a time, all the while knowing he had a serious girlfriend who lived in Washington, DC; he said he really liked me, and they were free to see other people, so I said to myself, why not? I knew I was not in love with him, but I did like him, and I loved his creativity, especially in bed! And it was cool dating him, because I went to some really great parties where I met some very famous musicians. My favorite ones would have to be David Lee Roth who was the lead singer from Van Halen. And John Taylor, the bass guitar player for Duran Duran. They were very fun to hang out and party with. I never told Steve Thompson about my near-death experience; I still wasn't comfortable talking about it to other people, as I had not really come to terms with it myself. But one night we were talking and he just happened to say he had already done everything he ever wanted to do in his life. There was just one thing left that he really wanted to do, he said, and that was to meet God. *I've got you beat there,* I thought to myself, *because I already did that!* Steve and I never really broke up; more like drifted away from each other, but still kept in touch as friends.

Then came Steve #2, as I like to call him. Steve #2 hit me like a tornado! He came whizzing into my life on June 14, 1987. I was now twenty years old, and was still modeling. I was now working as a ring card girl at Madison Square Garden in NYC. A ring girl is a young lady who enters the ring between boxing rounds carrying a sign that displays the number of the upcoming round. Tony Danza, and Burt Young used to be there watching the boxing matches. One night Burt Young who was Sylvester Stallone's brother-in-law in the movie *Rocky* came over to me, and handed me the key to his hotel room. He told me to meet him in his room later on that evening. I politely declined handing him his key back, and thought to myself if he was Sylvester Stallone I just might have taken him up on his offer! I had just started dating Steve who I was crazy about. He was twenty-five. We met at a nightclub on the water in Island Park called Channel 80, a place that was so hot it was always jam-packed and some nights it was hard to get in. People referred to it as Studio 54 on Long Island, that's how happening it was. On this particular evening, I went there with a bunch of friends, and I spotted him as soon as I walked in the door. He was wearing a suit and tie, and he looked a lot like Tony Danza. I had never done such a thing before, but when I walked by him, I gave him this come-hither look, and he nearly fell off his feet—at least that's what he pretended to do!

He beckoned me over to him, and the rest is history. I was completely smitten with him. He lived in Old Brookville, came from old money, and worked in his family's catering business. Whenever he wasn't working, we were together; he said we fit like the missing piece to a puzzle. We spent weekends together in Montauk out on the Island's tip, hanging out on the beach. We would talk for hours, and walk along the ocean together, then make love under the moon and stars. I was so sure I was in love with him, I wanted nothing more than to spend my life with him, making babies, and live happily ever after. Only it was not to be: he was Greek Orthodox, I was Jewish, and his dad forbade him to marry me or he would disown him. I cared so much about him that I couldn't bear to be the cause of that; I was afraid he might even come to resent me one day for tearing him from his family. So we broke up, and I was truly heartbroken, because I knew in my heart that it was really over—that even if we still had feelings for each other, our love was forbidden. Now I know that if we had gotten married all those years ago, it never would have worked out. We were two very different people. I was so spiritual and he wasn't and what I saw in him then, I wouldn't be interested in now. You see how God really does work in mysterious ways.

But at the time I was devastated, and there were many nights I cried myself to sleep. And who did I call? Ron! Now I know why: because my heart still belonged to him. I had not spoken to Ron in three years, and hearing his voice made me long for him, even as it comforted me. But it didn't last. "I can't talk for long," he said. He was moving to Chicago—literally, right then, that day. I'd caught him just as he was heading out the door. Now, with my failed love affair with Steve over and my Ron moving away, I was beyond down in the dumps. I thought to myself, *Can it possibly get any worse?*

Unfortunately, it could, and it did a couple of days after I called Ron. I was modeling at an auto show—hired to pose beside the cars and add a bit more sparkle, a fashion accessory, in other words!—when a very handsome guy approached me and started to flirt with me. He told me he would buy the car I was showing if I gave him my phone number. As physically attracted to him as I was, a chill went up my spine. I only had a bikini on, so I thought I must be cold. Now I know it was my guardian angels trying to steer me away from this handsome stranger!

Foolishly, I ignored the feeling. I gave him my number and we went out to dinner the very next night. He was twelve years older than me, thirty-four, and handsome enough to be a model or an actor himself—he looked a lot like Antonio Sabáto, Jr.— but it turned out he was actually a police officer. I figured that was even better! And I started to relax with him over dinner, because I thought I was in good hands. So when he invited me back to his place for a drink after dinner, I thought nothing of it. He was a cop; what could go wrong? Everything. As soon as the door closed behind us, he lunged at me and tore my dress off. Before I knew what was happening, he had me down on the bed, and I couldn't fight him off or even scream for help because he had me in a chokehold. While I gasped for air, he raped me. All I could think was *I'm going to die.* I really thought I wasn't going to survive this night. Then all of a sudden I remembered my angels in heaven warning me that I would go through something so awful I wouldn't think I could survive it—but I would, because they would be watching over me the whole time. When I remembered that, it comforted me a little, and I just prayed to God that this nightmare would end soon.

When it was over, he loosened his grip on my neck and took some pictures from underneath his bed—gruesome photos of a woman who had been stabbed to death. "See this?" he said. "If you tell anyone, this is what'll happen to you." I started to cry. I couldn't help it.

"Why?" I asked him. "You're a police officer. You're supposed to protect people, not hurt them!"

"I didn't do that to her," he said, pointing to the picture. "It was taken at a crime scene. I just want you to know that if you report me, I *will* hurt you." Then, as if nothing had happened at all, he said, "Do you want that drink now?"

I was still shaking and crying. "I want to leave right now," I said. So he drove me home. I had no other way to get there, not enough money in my purse for a cab, and I was so traumatized I could hardly think straight. When he dropped me off, he had the nerve to say he would call me again. The very next day I changed my phone number! "What happened to your neck?" my mother asked when I got inside and she saw the marks where he'd grabbed me. I started to sob again. Then I told her what had happened. She wanted to call his precinct and report him.

"No!" I screamed. "You can't!" I was so scared of those pictures he had shown me that I wouldn't let her pick up the phone. "I just want to forget about it." Maybe if I pretended it wasn't real, it would go away. But that was not to be.

A few weeks later I realized I was pregnant—a painful reminder of just how real it was. Somehow, though, I started to think of it as something of a blessing, something good coming out of the bad. I decided I wanted to keep the baby. Even *that* was not to be. I had been wearing so much makeup when I was modeling that my skin had begun to break out, and my dermatologist put me on Accutane. It made my skin flawless, peaches and cream, but it came with a warning on it, not to get pregnant while using it, as it could cause deformities in the fetus. My gynecologist said to me that I could not under any circumstances have this baby, that it would be born missing arms or legs or both. He showed me pictures of babies born to mothers who'd been taking the drug, and all of them were terribly deformed. As sad as I was, I knew I had to do what was best for my baby; I couldn't bring a child into the world just to suffer, when I of all people knew how beautiful heaven was.

I knew I had made the right decision, but just the same, it was with a heavy heart that I terminated the pregnancy. It was early on, and I was able to have a D&C, a simple procedure; but still, as I lay there on the table while my baby was being taken from me, I couldn't help feeling violated all over again, almost like a second rape.

All of a sudden I felt something touching my hair, like a gentle hand. I looked around, but no one was there. Then I realized it was my angels stroking my hair the way they said they would whenever I was feeling lonely, to let me know they were with me always. I remembered how they'd told me that once I got through the terrible thing I didn't think I would survive, I would never go through anything like that again, and I would always be okay.

After that, I could no longer push away the thoughts of heaven. It seemed closer than ever to me, as I visualized my baby there, happy and whole. I received confirmation of this when one night I awoke from my sleep feeling a strong presence in my bedroom. I opened my eyes to find my beautiful baby—now my baby angel, with delicate little wings, holding a small magic wand—gazing down at me. We smiled at each other, and my precious baby angel then waved its wand at me once more before leaving. Tears welled up in my eyes; to think that my baby angel had come to me to reassure me it was happy was beyond comforting to me. It gave me the strength to carry on. I came out of this sad, lonely time in my life more determined than ever to seek answers to the questions I had.

I started to think seriously about my near-death experience and read everything I could about other people's. Lots of people had gone through that tunnel, met loved ones, and seen angels, but I didn't find any other stories of meeting God in person. Why had I been singled out? And why did bad things sometimes happen to good people? I was ready to turn to God and make sense of it all. And, slowly but surely, the answers started to come. My real spiritual journey was about to begin.

Chapter 10

God's Light and Love

When I made the choice to come back from heaven, I was doing it mostly because I thought my mother needed me. I had seen her anguish in the vision of my funeral, and I just couldn't let her live with that pain. The angels had told me that my mother and I would always have a special connection with each other. We'd finish each other's sentences; sometimes we'd even know what the other was thinking. But they also said that our relationship would sometimes be rocky—"no bed of roses" is how they put it—and boy, did they turn out to be right. Not that God's angels could be wrong!

This all proved true a few years after my parents got divorced—that had happened when I was eighteen. Now I was living with my mother in a two-bedroom apartment in Freeport when my mom started dating a man whom I didn't like from the start. This man, Gary, felt threatened by seeing just how close she and I were, not just mother and daughter, but best friends too. He cornered me one day when my mom was out of the room and told me point-blank that he was going to do everything he could to break our relationship apart. And that's exactly what he did: he tore us apart.

Naturally, I told my mother what he had said, but she dismissed it. "He didn't really mean that," she said. "He's just a little possessive." She said it was because he loved her so much that he didn't want anyone else to be close to her. That didn't sound much like love to me, but I guess she had rose-colored glasses on, or should I say blinders? At the very least, she couldn't or didn't want to see him for what he really was, which was not a very nice guy. Anyone who would want to tear a mother and daughter apart, especially when he knew that I barely had a relationship with my father and she was all I had, can't be too kind. I secretly hoped they would break up, but they didn't. In fact, only a couple of months into their courtship, Gary moved in with us. You can imagine what an uncomfortable situation that was for me in a two-bedroom apartment, with no privacy from this intolerable man I hardly knew (and didn't want to know)!

From the moment he moved in, he kept telling my mother that I needed to move out. He even went as far as to tell her that he wouldn't marry her unless she threw me out. For a while she tried to stick up for me. "I can't throw Elissa out," she'd say. "She doesn't have any place else to go." Then one day he gave her an ultimatum: me or him. If she chose him, I couldn't live with them anymore, and if she chose me, he would leave her. My poor mother was in tears, but she told him, "You are asking me the unthinkable. I cannot throw my daughter out in the street, and you should not make me have to choose between the two of you." Still he held his ground. Finally my mother came to her senses and said, "I will not throw my child out." She "chose" me! Gary moved out, and I thought that was the end of him. I was so happy that our relationship was back to normal and our home was filled with peace once again.

A couple of days after he moved out, I met a new man of my own. His name was Freddy, and we met at a nightclub in the Garden City Hotel. At first he seemed like a nice change after the trauma I had been through of being raped and then losing my baby. Like a gentleman, he didn't pressure me for sex; he said, "I want a full relationship with you."

When we started dating, it was hard for my mother, because she was vulnerable after losing Gary in the choice between him and me. Once she saw that I was dating someone, she started to weaken. "Maybe I should call Gary," she kept saying. "Maybe I should work things out with him."

You have to understand that my mother was not a strong

woman emotionally, which was why I always felt more like I was her mother than the other way around! I pleaded with her not to; I told her it would be a huge mistake, and I reassured her that she'd definitely made the right decision to let it end. I told her she deserved a much kinder man, one who would treat her properly and not try to control her. I also assured her that it wasn't serious with Freddy, just casual dating, and she had nothing to worry about—I wasn't going to up and leave her to be with Freddy. Because I knew she felt that if I was going to move in with my boyfriend, then she should not have broken off with hers.

I thought I had succeeded in reassuring her, but I was wrong. Three months into dating Freddy, I realized that he was definitely not the right person for me. He was too moody, too quiet; he seemed like an unhappy person, and he was making me unhappy too. We had gone out to dinner and to see a movie, and in the theater, while we were watching Warren Beatty and Annette Bening in *Bugsy*, I decided that I would break up with him when he drove me home that night. Well, talk about lousy timing. I was going to tell Freddy once we got inside that I thought we should stop seeing each other. But when I put my key in the door, it wouldn't turn. I kept trying, and Freddy tried too, but the door wouldn't open. Then all of a sudden someone inside the apartment pulled it open. It was Gary, standing next to my mother with a smug look on his face. "Your mother and I are back together," he said to me. "We're engaged, and we're going to get married. We changed the locks. You have to find another place to live." I felt as if I had just been kicked in the gut, *and* I was homeless on top of it. Here I was about to break up with Freddy, and now I've been evicted in the middle of the night with no place to go!

My mother started to choke up, but you could see that she had already been brainwashed by this cruel man. "I'm sorry, Elissa," was all she said. "Go with Freddy. He'll take care of you." Talk about being between a rock and a hard place! Before I could even answer, Freddy turned to me and said, "You can move in with me. I was planning on asking you to marry me anyway." Not exactly what I wanted to hear from the man I was about to break up with! But it was the middle of the night, and I had no place else to go, so I thought I had no choice. I took him up on his offer and moved in. A year later we were married. I was twenty-six years old.

So this was what the angels meant. I didn't speak to my mother after that night for almost a year. I felt so hurt and betrayed that I had chosen to come back for my mother when I was in heaven, and then she turned around and chose someone else over me. "This is what I came back for?" I yelled at her before Gary closed the door. "I was so peaceful in heaven, what the hell did I need to come back to you for?" I was angry when I said that, but a part of me really wondered. Why *had* I come back? What was the purpose that God sent me back for? Was it just so that I could lose my mother and marry a man I didn't love? Then something else happened. My beloved grandmother was diagnosed with cancer and given six months to live.

Remember, my grandmother had had a near-death experience of her own; she'd made that trip through the tunnel and into the light, where her loved ones met her and told her it wasn't her time. So she knew a little bit about heaven. But she hadn't seen and experienced all that I had seen, and as her time neared, I knew that she was terrified to die. More than anything, she feared that this death would be painful, because of the cancer. I remembered telling my friend Amy about my trip to heaven right after it happened. I remembered that after hearing it, Amy said she wouldn't be afraid to die any more. Of course, Amy was a teenager in perfect health, and teenagers think they're immortal anyway! But even so, I wondered if my story might help my grandmother, too, to see that death was nothing to fear.

So one afternoon I sat on my grandmother's bed and told her

again about heaven. I reminded her of what she'd seen herself, then I told her what *I* knew—that there was no pain, and that her guardian angels would be waiting for her in the light of heaven, and that her own beloved mother, whom she had mourned for so long, would be waiting for her there. When I finished, her eyes were filled with tears. "You're an evangelist," she said. Then she thanked me for calming her fear. She told me she was ready to go to heaven after what I'd told her. Finally, she told me she loved me. And when she did pass away some time later, the look on her face was one of perfect peace. I was happy to know that she was once again embraced by the light. And I was happy to be reminded of something I had known all along, ever since I died and went to heaven and was enveloped in God's light and love there.

I knew—I know—that *everything* is centered in God's light and love. We are all part of that light. Our souls are made up of light, and our hearts are its home, where we store all the love that comes from that light. Without it, there would be no love, and without any love, there would be no life. That's why it saddens me when a tragedy occurs in someone's life and I hear them say they have lost their faith in God. You must never turn your back on God, because God *never* turns His back on you. It is in your darkest hour that He is with you the most. I prefer to think of it as a test of faith, that God may be testing your strength of character, testing to see who will turn to Him and who will turn away.

I can never forget the Connecticut mother who lost all of her children early one Christmas morning when a fire broke out in the house. Some said her three little girls were concerned that Santa might get burned coming down the chimney; in a tragic twist, it was thought (though never proven) that the embers from that same fire, disposed of improperly, sparked the blaze that claimed their lives. Never once did I hear that poor grieving mother blame God. Instead, she thanked Him for having been blessed with the time she was granted with them. She did ask, why did this happen to her? and why were her three beautiful daughters' lives cut so short? But she never blamed God or turned her back on Him.

Or the heartbreaking, unspeakable tragedy of twenty precious, innocent children being gunned down in their classroom at Sandy Hook Elementary School in Newtown, Connecticut. A total of twenty-six people lost their lives that day, when a mentally disturbed twenty-year-old man gunned them down just as a new school day was beginning. I cried for each and every single one of those precious children who lost their lives. What astounded me, though, was the courage, strength, and deep faith in God that one of the mothers had who lost her beautiful child. She said, "I was raised, and went on to raise my family, not to have any hatred in our hearts or our home." She said, "Even though we are deeply grieving for our loss, we don't have any hatred toward the gunman who did this." I know this woman must be a very spiritual being and have a close relationship with God to feel this way. It is God's light and love in her that shields her from feeling such hatred.

On the other side, a good friend of mine is struggling to come to terms with her son having been diagnosed with muscular dystrophy. She is so heartbroken over it that she tells me she no longer believes in God. She just doesn't believe in anything anymore. While my heart goes out to her for her son, as no mother can bear to see her child suffer, it breaks my heart just as much, if not more, that she has given up on God. When you do that, a light goes out inside of you, and you die. You may still be here in a physical sense, but spiritually, you're gone. I wish I could shake my friend and make her realize that she needs God more than ever now. We all have to have suffering in our lifetime—without it we can't grow spiritually. No one ever said it was going to be a walk in the park or a trip to Disney World! Life is hard, life is work—a course that your soul signed up for before you came here. Every person on the face of this earth was involved in charting their own lives, step by step, every second of their lives planned out. Didn't my guardian angels tell me, when I went to heaven, that everything is already written in the book? God does not give us anything more than we can handle, and His light is always inside us, even in our darkest hour.

There's a famous poem called "Footprints in the Sand," which talks about a person's life as a line of footprints along a beach. Most of the time there are two sets of prints — the person's and God's — but sometimes there is just one set, and those match up with the hardest times in the person's life. In the poem, the person cries out to God, "Why did you leave me when I needed you the most?" And God replies, "I never left you, my child. Those places where you see one set of footprints — that was when I carried you." I'll say it again: God does not give you more than you can handle. You may think he does, but he knows your soul — he created it — and he knows just what you are capable of.

Sometimes what seems like misfortune is really payment for a past life's karma; the laws of karma are strong, and there is both good and bad, and I can assure you that what goes around really does come around. A friend of mine was in a terrible car accident when he was eighteen years old, struck head-on by a truck while he was driving home from college in a blizzard. He broke his neck and severely injured his spine, and now he is paralyzed from the waist down, and it's unlikely he will ever walk again. He told me that he too had a glimpse of heaven in a near-death experience during his accident; while he didn't meet God as I did, he met an angel, who told him that this was happening to him because in a past life he was a gladiator and killed another person in a fight. The angel said he was being sent back to his life to live it out handicapped to pay for that old karma. My friend accepted his fate, and instead of being upset with God, he loves God more than ever.

And what about me? Instead of being upset with God when I was date-raped, asking why that happened and why I wasn't allowed to keep my baby, I just kept praying to Him that when the time was right He would send a healthy baby to me.

One day while I was meditating, the most beautiful thing happened. God showed me a healthy, precious baby girl, letting me know that He *would* send her to me when the time was right. Five years later, I gave birth to that healthy, precious baby girl! She looked exactly like the baby God showed me. I named her Raphaela, which is a very spiritual name; it means, "God has healed," and it's also the name of one of God's highest archangels.

Right after I gave birth to Raphaela in the hospital, I went to visit her in the maternity ward. All of the newborn babies were lined up in the nursery, in their bassinets, with their heads facing the other way, so I couldn't tell which one was her. All of a sudden a bright beam of light shot out from me, straight through the glass partition and right to the back of one baby's head. I knew it was God's light and love pouring out from me to her, letting me know that was my baby girl—my angel. Sure enough, it was Raphaela.

Chapter 11

Peace, Purpose, and Divine Awareness

Do you ever notice how when you're doing what you're meant to be doing, everything just seems to fall into place? Versus how, when you're doing something you know you shouldn't be doing, it all seems to fall apart! That's how you can tell if you are living your life in line with God's purpose for you. This is true of work, for certain: I know so many people who are miserable and feel as if they're in dead-end jobs, simply because they can't stand the work that they do. My answer to that is always the same: change the line of work you're in! If you do what you enjoy, you won't even see it as work, but as something that fulfills you from deep within your soul. You'll be living a life of authentic power and self-awareness, which is the same thing as divine awareness: exactly what we all need in order to live the way God intends us to and fulfill our own purpose here on earth.

Here's a perfect example of how things can fall into place. I started working in dog rescue after I got married, about ten years before I had Raphaela, volunteering at shelters and finding homes for animals that were going to be euthanized otherwise. I'll never forget the beautiful Doberman pinscher that showed up on my doorstep when I was eighteen years old, near collapse, with a bullet in her back. It sickened me that anyone could be so cruel to a beautiful, defenseless animal—a beautiful soul that gives nothing but unconditional love. Because she didn't belong to anyone in my neighborhood, I had to assume that God sent her to me to help—which of course I did.

On Christmas Eve 2000, I came across another Doberman, this time a precious ten-month-old red Doberman puppy, that was about to be put to sleep at a kill shelter in Queens. This poor dog was in a cage so small he couldn't stand up in it, and when I asked how long he'd been in there, they told me ten days. Then they told me that if no one took the dog that day, he would be euthanized before they closed that night. "I'll take him," I said at once. I knew there was no way this gorgeous puppy's time on earth was meant to be over yet! When I had filled out the paperwork and it was time to leave, I had never seen a dog as ecstatic to be let out of a cage before in my life! To say he was wild would be an understatement. Bouncing off the walls was more like it! But who could blame him, after not being able to stand up for ten days?

So now here I was, out on the street with a ten-month-old Doberman puppy that had more pent-up energy than either of us knew what to do with. What did I do? Get him in my car as fast as I could! All the shelter had given me for him was a rope that served as a leash. Well, that didn't last very long. The energetic pup used the rope as a chew toy and chewed it to pieces within minutes. Then he started doing the same thing to my seatbelts. I didn't have the heart to scold him, after the ordeal he had just been through, but I realized he was too wild for me to safely drive home with him.

I got out of the car, leaving the dog still chewing on the seatbelts, and just as I got out, I saw a police car driving past. I waved and motioned for him to pull over. When he pulled up in front of my car and got out, I let out a huge sigh of relief. I just knew this policeman was going to be able to help me. When I told him my story, he said, "I don't believe it. I have a red Doberman puppy too. They're the best dogs." "Well, this one is in need of some major training," I said, "because he is chewing up all of the seatbelts in my car." By this time he had climbed up front and was working on the front seatbelts! The cop laughed. "Don't worry," he said. "I won't give you a ticket for not wearing your seatbelt!" "Please help me," I said. I told him I didn't have a leash for the puppy and he'd chewed right through the rope the shelter gave me. The policeman said no problem—he had an extra collar and leash in the trunk of his car that he'd bought on his lunch break that day for his own dog. He even had some dog food—music to my ears! As soon as the officer put the collar and leash on the puppy and took him out of the car, he was still excited, but much calmer than he had been.

While the dog was eating dog food (instead of my seatbelts), I put a call in to a friend, who said he wanted to adopt the puppy and surprise his nine-year-old nephew with it for Christmas the next day. "That's great," I said. "Could you get here as quick as you can, before he eats my entire car?" Sure enough, my friend showed up half an hour later, and as soon as the dog saw him, he stood up on him and licked his face. I wanted to say, "I'll send you a bill for my car," but I knew the dog wouldn't understand! Then I turned to the policeman and thanked him for all of his help. I knew that his showing up at the exact time I needed him, with everything we needed to help the dog, was no coincidence; it was all a part of God's bigger plan, things falling into place for a purpose. And I felt so good that I was able to make that an extra-special Christmas for a boy and his dog!

In the years after my near-death experience, I did an enormous amount of soul-searching, trying to discern what my own purpose was to be. I knew God had sent me back with a purpose—he told me so—I just didn't know what it was! He had told me it would be revealed in time, so I just had to trust that it would. Then, when I was forty-three years old, I woke up one night in the grip of a flashback. I often remembered my near-death experience—I thought about it a lot—but this was different. This time I started to recall more of it—something about what my purpose for being sent back here was. I was standing beside God as He watched over the world, and He was telling me something. Something about a messenger—that I would be *His* messenger—an angel sent by Him to deliver an important message from Him! While it still wasn't crystal-clear, I was certain about that much, and I knew that the rest of whatever that important purpose was, whatever God wanted me to do for Him here on earth, would reveal itself soon now.

I was elated that the time was finally coming that God had prepared me for all these years, saying that He would reveal my purpose for being sent back when the time was right and I was mature enough to handle it; it was finally here! Now I was allowed to remember I was sent back to deliver a message. The only other thing I needed to know was what was that message? Once again, I knew that would be revealed to me when the time was right. Talk about being kept in suspense! As intrigued as I was, my faith in God told me to trust in His will. He would reveal my purpose to me on His terms, and that was good enough for me!

Not long after that, I had a dream about my grandmother, Lily, who died at peace after we talked about heaven together. In my dream she said to me, "You have done all of your soul-searching already, and done as much of it as you can possibly do. Now it is time to just be." I woke up the next morning and understood the message she had sent to me in my dream: that it was time to take all the lessons I had learned and apply them to my life, to really live my life to the fullest extent. Because my grandmother knew as well as I did that I was not reaching my full potential! I had all the answers I needed inside of me, yet when push came to shove, I was still allowing people to make the wrong decisions for me. Once I realized that you really are the captain of your own ship, I realized it was time to jump ship in another sense. Not in a physical sense, of course—in a spiritual manner, I'm talking! And for me, the ship I had to jump was my marriage.

When I first got married, there were many signs that indicated to me that this person was not the man I wanted to spend the rest of my life with. But since I was young when I got married—only twenty-six—I chose to ignore those signs, and I tried my best to make it work. There were ups and downs, but, truth be told, far too many downs, and many times I felt I was walking on eggshells. I kept telling myself, *Things will get better.* I always hoped that my husband would change, that he'd be more of the man I wanted and needed him to be. But a leopard doesn't change its spots, and Freddy did not change either.

For a long time, I believed I could *help* him become a better man, and I sacrificed a lot of myself to try and "save" him. But the kinder I was to him, the more abusive he was to me. I was weak physically, and my husband knew that and drew upon it. He instilled the fear in me that I would never be able to survive without him—not physically and certainly not financially. He controlled all the finances, which in his mind was the perfect way of keeping me from leaving him. He was a wealthy man, but he kept me on a tight leash. What he didn't know was how strong my spirit was. He may have been physically stronger than me, but he was no match for me spiritually. Spiritually, I was fierce! And like a caged lion when it's held in captivity too long, it's going to pounce all over you once it gets out of that cage! My husband tried to break me, and in some ways he did, but the one thing he could never break was my spirit. He was such an unhappy person that he wanted to make me as unhappy as he was, and he did, in every way, except in my spirit.

I never lost my faith in God, as I knew that God did not choose me to stand before Him in heaven and send me back with an important purpose all for nothing. I knew that everything I was going through was going to lead me to a better place when the time was right. I even thought that maybe He was testing me to see how strong I really was and how much I could endure before He revealed my purpose to me.

Looking back, I can see that I stayed with my husband for far too long. I ignored my strong intuition that we weren't meant to be together—and intuition is just another form of divine awareness! Think of your intuition as your best friend, a guide that helps you live your life in line with your purpose. It's truly a gift from God, one that gives you signs to let you know when you are on the right path as well as when you're on the wrong one. Sometimes intuition is a warning, and then you ignore it at your own risk.

While I was writing this book, my daughter went to a Fourth of July beach barbecue; one of her friends' dads had a small boat there, and my daughter wanted so badly to go out on it to watch the fireworks over the Long Island Sound. I felt it was too small, not safe. As her eyes welled up with tears, to accompany her nonstop pleas of "Please, Mom" and "You're ruining my life!" —I was thinking, *No I'm not—I just might be saving it!* But she won out and I gave in. With a heavy heart (and a life jacket) I let her go on the boat, as long as my husband went with her to make sure she was okay, because I am afraid of small boats myself and won't go on anything smaller than a cruise ship! Thankfully, my daughter made it back to shore safe and sound, but another boat near them wasn't as fortunate. This other boat was much bigger, but even so it capsized, and three children were trapped in the cabin and drowned. Two of the three lived in my town, and to make it even more tragic, it was the birthday of one of the girls. She had turned eight that day, on July 4, and she'd pleaded with her mom to let her go see the fireworks for her birthday. A friend of mine, who was good friends with that little girl's mother, went to the funeral, and she said she heard her crying that she'd had a feeling they should not go on the boat. She almost called up at the last minute to cancel. But in the end she went against what her intuition was telling her, and they went on that fateful boat ride after all. You can be sure that I gave my daughter the biggest hug when I tucked her into bed that night, thanking God that she was all right, and said a prayer for the families who'd lost their precious children.

I remember a time in my life when I knew I had to follow the signs I was being given, even though they went against what I thought I wanted. It was when my daughter was a toddler and we were living in a gated community on the beach. This was on the South Shore of Long Island, right on the Atlantic Ocean, which has the most beautiful sandy beaches. In fact, our town was Atlantic Beach! I got pregnant with Raphaela and gave birth to her while we were living there, and my fondest memories are of strolling her in her baby stroller right along the ocean, hearing the sound of the waves crashing on the sand, lulling my baby to sleep. It was beautiful and peaceful, and those were my most precious moments with her. I wished those days could go on forever. If only life worked that way—but reality set in, and one day my husband, who always seemed to enjoy raining on my parade, said, "I think it's time we moved." He said that now that our daughter was getting bigger, we should move to a better school district, as the one we were living in was terrible and if we stayed she'd have to go to private school. Which we would have sent her to, if we had stayed there.

But fate had other plans for us, and one day there was an ad in the real-estate section of the newspaper that caught my husband's eye. He said, "This sounds like the house we've been waiting to go on the market." I grabbed the paper from him, and sure enough, that was the same address as a house we'd been driving by and admiring for the past five years! It was a large Mediterranean villa right on the water in the town of Lloyd Harbor, and it even had—my favorite part—a large indoor pool. But as much as I loved it, and I did, my heart was already attached to the home we were in, where my daughter had come into our lives.

I loved our South Shore beach; this house was on the North Shore, on the Long Island Sound, which I always thought of as the fake beach, because there was hardly any sand, mostly rocks, and you didn't have the big waves or hear the sound of the surf. And I had really come to love our gated development, where everyone was so friendly and we were all connected to one another by the peaceful beach lifestyle we had come to know. Even though the other house was in a development too, it was on a couple of acres, and it seemed isolated. Where we lived, there were always kids riding their bicycles and playing basketball in each other's driveways. There, I did not see one kid playing outdoors. Secretly I was hoping I wouldn't really like the house, but I said to myself, there isn't any harm in looking — and sure enough, it was the most beautiful house I had ever been inside of!

My husband assured me that Raphaela would still have kids to play with. "When it's estate living like this, people make play dates for their kids," he said. "You drive them to each other's houses." So we made an offer on the house, with part of me still hoping they wouldn't accept our offer. Then we waited. And one night I was in my bedroom when all of a sudden a beam of light shot out from the panel in the wall where the burglar alarm was. A voice said, "Elissa, the light will lead you wherever you need to go." The next morning — I wasn't dreaming — my grandmother appeared, floating above my bed. She said, "In case you're wondering where you should move to" — and she pointed to her own neck. Then she smiled at me and she was gone.

It only took me a moment to realize what she was saying. The house we had made the offer on was in an area of town called Lloyd Neck, the farthest tip of Lloyd Harbor. We always referred to it as the house in the Neck. We'd say to each other, "Should we move to the Neck?" I ran out of the room, yelling to my husband, "We have to move to the Neck! My grandmother just came and told me to move there. It's a sign we have to listen to!" No sooner had the words left my mouth than the telephone rang. It was the realtor calling to tell us that the sellers had accepted our offer. The house was ours! The last sign we received about our new house came after we went into contract.

My husband went to the house to pick up the keys to the gate, and when he looked at them, he said, "Look at the numbers on these keys!" The numbers were the same as my husband's birth date.

I knew you couldn't ignore signs like these, and whatever the reason, we did need to move there. So I did move, with a heavy heart even though I'd seen the signs. And it wasn't easy at first. Many days I missed my old place at the beach, and I know my little girl did too. It broke my heart to see her sitting all alone on the patio looking so forlorn, while I pictured all the kids back in our old community, whom I knew she would have been playing with at that very moment. It got so bad that one day I went to a well-known psychic to see if I should move back. "You're psychic yourself," was the first thing she said to me. "Why are you here?" I had to laugh. "I know!" I said. "But I need some extra help." Then she told me that I had indeed made the right move—that not only did she see better opportunities for my daughter living in our new place, but deeper involvement for me too.

Sure enough, a couple of months later a lovely family moved in across the street from us, with two children close to my daughter's age. It turned out that their mother grew up in Oceanside just like me; I didn't know her, because she was four years younger, but I lived across the street from her best friend at the time. Now we live across the street from each other and *we* have become best friends! Perhaps one day I will see a sign telling me to move back to my old home on the beach—hello, Grandma?—but for now my daughter is happy where we are. In that case, I followed the signs I was given.

When it came to my marriage, it took me a lot longer. Then the turning point came. I woke up one day in so much pain that I cried out to God, "Why are you doing this to me? I'm not as strong as you think. Can't you lighten the load a little bit? Even murderers get paroled after twenty years in prison, and I never murdered anyone. All I'm guilty of is making the wrong decision to come back to my life. Why are you punishing me?" As soon as I said that, I knew the answer. God wasn't punishing me, I was punishing myself. In my heart I knew I was the only one to blame, the only one responsible for keeping me in such a loveless marriage. The only one trapping me in it was me. "Please help me," I cried to God again. "I need your love and light to lead me out of this." I prayed for the strength and courage that I needed to live my life on my own. As soon as I did that, all my darkness turned to light. Once again I felt this surge of energy go through me, just as I did when I came back from heaven. It almost made me laugh that I had let a miserable bully control me for so long. The very next day I separated from my husband, and I knew I was heading down the right path—a path of clarity and confidence, peace and purpose, and above all a path of love. The purpose of your life is to learn how to make God's will your will. The goal in your life is to grow into an understanding of the Creator by shedding your ego, your shell, and reaching out to Him. The only truly important work is to have a more intimate relationship with God.

Chapter 12

The Gift of Forgiveness

I am a firm believer in forgiveness. I always say, if someone who was close to you or had any meaning in your life does you wrong—as long as they didn't kill anyone—then you should forgive them if you can find it in your heart, because life is simply too short to hold a grudge. What if you have a change of heart and it's too late? You may not be ready to let them back into your life the way you did before whatever it was took place—the relationship may be too damaged to repair fully—but just letting them know that you forgive them will not only lighten their load a bit, it will lighten yours as well. Do you ever notice, when you make up with someone, how you feel a little lighter right away, like a weight's been lifted off your shoulder? That is actually your soul cleansing itself, filtering out all of its toxic waste—its negative energy. It's much harder to carry around all of that dark energy inside of you than it is to set it free. When I forgive someone, I call it a spiritual cleansing. It's one of the healthiest things that you can do for yourself and your soul.

A couple of months ago I had a big falling-out with the mother of one of my daughter's friends. We had arranged a play date for our girls, and I had put a note in Raphaela's backpack that day telling the teacher that Abbey was to come home with Raphaela on the school bus. But just as the bus was about to leave, the teacher ran up and told Abbey that she had to get off. That the play date was cancelled and her mother was taking her home.

A few minutes after Raphaela got home from school, Abbey's mother called me very upset that I had put that note in my daughter's backpack. Apparently she had forgotten all about the play date, but instead of apologizing for her oversight, she was blaming me for her own irresponsibility! She said she got very scared when she went to pick Abbey up from school and she wasn't in the usual place. "I'm sorry you got scared," I said, "but I didn't do anything wrong." I resisted the temptation to add, *But you did!* My daughter's teacher even called her up to say that she owed me an apology. This mom, though, was very stubborn and refused to give in. In the meantime, both our daughters were upset, as they were good friends, and now they weren't going over to each other's houses to play after school. I felt bad for my daughter, but I knew I was really in the right, and I was waiting for the other mother to apologize to me.

Well, days turned into weeks, and still no apology. Then one night my daughter's friend Abbey came to me in a dream. She said, "Could you please call my mother? She really wants to apologize to you, but she's afraid to make the first move." When I woke up the next morning, I thought how sad this little girl must be if she had to reach out to me in a dream. I knew it was a sign I shouldn't ignore. I picked up the phone to dial. All right, I'll admit that I hung up the first time, fearing she might hang up on *me*. But I took a deep breath and dialed again, and when she answered, I told her about the dream I'd had.

"I am so glad you called," she said. "I picked up the phone so many times to call you, but I never had the guts to go through with it!" She said she was afraid that I wouldn't accept her apology and might even hang up on her. So we both had the same fear! When I got off the phone, the whole issue was resolved and we'd both apologized to each other, and I felt so much lighter. In that instant I realized it didn't matter who was right and who was wrong. All that mattered to me was that we were friends once again, and our daughters were too.

A few years earlier, I'd had a misunderstanding with another mom that turned into an even bigger rift. I knew this woman from Oceanside because like me she grew up there. But she was a few years younger than me. Her mother had owned a nail salon in Oceanside, and I had even done some hand modeling for her. At the time, her twins were in the same preschool class as my daughter, and she used to drop them off and pick them up every day. Then she stopped appearing, and I didn't see her at school for a long time. One day, out of concern, I said to one of the twins, "Where is your mom?" The little girl said to me, "She fell and broke her back, and she can't drive us anymore." Just then the twins' nanny overheard me speaking to the little girl and told her not to say another word. I felt that was a little odd, and it seemed odder still when I got a phone call that evening from the twins' mother, Julie, "How dare you corner my child and ask her all sorts of questions about me?" "Julie," I said, "I only asked out of concern why you don't come to school anymore. I think that's a normal question to ask?"

"It's none of your business," she said, and hung up on me! The very next day at school, her daughter said to Raphaela, "My mom doesn't want me to play with you anymore, because she doesn't like your mom." I was so shocked by this—and I felt so bad for my daughter, who was upset, as she and the other girl had been good friends—that when I went home that day I called Julie and left a message on her answering machine. I said, "Julie, I think when you fell and hurt your back, you also must have hit your head, because you're not acting in your right mind! How dare you have your child tell my daughter she can't play with her because you don't like me? If you have an issue with me, you take it up privately with me—you don't drag our kids into it." Then I hung up feeling proud of myself for standing up for my child and myself.

A few weeks later I happened to be talking to another mother at our preschool. When I asked her where she'd grown up, she said, "Oceanside." I know, small world! When I asked her if she knew Julie, she exclaimed, "Oh my God! That was my best friend from childhood and all through high school." Neither of them had any clue that they lived near each other again and their kids went to the same preschool. We agreed that they'd probably passed each other in the hall many times and not recognized each other. "Here's Julie's phone number," I said. "Call her." And the other woman, Donna, said she would. The next day at school, Donna told me that she and Julie had spoken for two hours and that she was going over to Julie's house that day to see her. Again she thanked me for reuniting her with her old friend.

It wasn't until a couple of months later that I found out through another friend that Julie hadn't really fallen and hurt her back at all, as her little girl had told me. It was much more serious than that. Julie really had lung cancer, and she was now on her deathbed. I was stunned, because Julie was such a health fanatic; I knew she'd never smoked, and she ate very healthy and exercised religiously. My hand flew up to my mouth as I cried, "I don't believe it! I am so sorry!" Then I immediately thought back to the fight that we'd had and the nasty message I'd left for her, saying I thought she must have fallen on her head too. Even though at the time I'd felt I had every reason to do that, as she had hurt my daughter's feelings, I knew that I needed to call her to apologize now.

So I called again, but again she didn't pick up; this time, I thought, she was probably too weak to talk on the phone. Instead I left another message, only this one was filled with compassion. I told her I only wished her and her family the best, and I hoped she could forgive me for the message I had left her months earlier—that it was only out of hurt I'd said those things to her. I said that life is just too short to hold a grudge—maybe not the best choice of words for a dying woman? I even told her a little about my near-death experience, hoping that maybe she wouldn't be afraid to die. Then I said, "God bless you," and hung up, feeling better that I'd tried to make my peace with her.

A couple of days later, I heard that Julie had passed away. I felt so bad for her little twins that I cried; it broke my heart that they would grow up without their mother. I cried all weekend long. Then on Monday at preschool, Donna came up to me. She was crying too, and she said to me, "I have a message from Julie for you." She said that Julie could only speak in a whisper for the last week of her life, but she told Donna that she'd heard my message on her answering machine, and she not only forgave me—she told Donna to thank me for bringing her friend back into her life again. She said that it was the best gift I could have given her before she died. Donna said that they both thought of me as an angel for bringing them together again. I thought, *If they only knew!*

When I think about forgiveness, I can't help thinking about something very close to home—my dad. I walked around for many years truly believing that he must be a terrible person, because I figured if he wasn't a good husband or a good father, then it stood to reason that he wasn't a good person either. While I wouldn't say that I hated him, I certainly couldn't tell you that I liked him very much. In fact, after my parents got divorced when I was eighteen, we were pretty thoroughly estranged for several years after that. I wasn't sure if I would ever see him again, or if I even wanted to.

Then one day out of the blue I got a letter from him in the mail. He told me that he had moved to Florida after the divorce, and that he had many regrets about the kind of father he had been. He said that even though he'd never win a Father of the Year award, he was truly sorry that he wasn't a good dad to me, and if I could find it in my heart to forgive him, he would try to make it up to me now. He was never shown any love or affection growing up, he explained, and he didn't know how to be a father himself, but through therapy and reading he was making progress within himself now, and he would love nothing more than to have some kind of relationship with me.

At first I thought to myself, *Talk about too little too late.* But then I started to soften a little. I tried to think of anything positive that had ever come out of him being my dad. At first nothing was coming to mind, just a little girl wishing she had a nice daddy who really loved her. But then I had a vision of my beloved, beautiful German shorthaired pointer Shag, who was a surprise for the whole family from my dad on Valentine's Day.

That's it, I thought. *I did receive some of the love that he found it so hard to show me when he brought this special dog into my life for fourteen wonderful years.* Shag and I had such a bond with each other that the day he had to be put to sleep, because he was having terrible seizures and trouble breathing, he would not leave the house until he came to me to say goodbye. I heard a scratch at my bedroom door, and when I opened it and looked into his eyes, our eyes pierced each other's souls. He knew as well as I did that he was leaving and not coming back. I leaned down and whispered in his ear, "It's okay, Shag, I know it's your time to go. I love you and always will." Then I said, "Go have peace in heaven." I knew that it was a gift from Shag that he was letting me know how much he loved me too, and I realized now that it was because of my dad I'd had that love.

That was the truth in my heart that I needed to find in order to forgive my dad. I knew he needed my forgiveness, and I decided to give him that gift. He still might not win that Father of the Year award, but we do have a relationship, or at least we're working on it! He walked me down the aisle when I got married, and he has met my daughter; in fact, she's helping me make a surprise eightieth birthday party for him. I know when we forgive—or do any act of kindness—it puts a smile on God's face.

And what about my mother, who threw me out and changed the locks? She did betray me and hurt me deeply, but I knew that if God could give me the gift of my life back, I could give her the gift of forgiveness just like I did my dad. Standing before God in heaven, feeling his light and love pour through me, made it much easier for me to forgive them both, as God is forgiveness itself. My mother and I made up with each other when I got pregnant several months after she evicted me. I was so excited to become a mother, and I desperately wanted to share this good news with my mom. I was still upset with her for what she did to me, but I started to weaken, and I found myself calling her one day to let her know she was going to become a grandmother. She started to cry. "I'm so happy for you," she said. "I'm going to ask Gary if I can be a part of your life and the baby's life." Obviously she was still being controlled by him! But the next day she called back and said that he was actually loosening the reins a bit now, and she would be able to see me.

As it turned out, I had a miscarriage and lost that baby, so my mother had to wait ten more years for me to get pregnant with Raphaela. It took a long time for us to get our relationship back on track, as I was still hurt by what she had done to me, pushing me to marry Freddy when she knew full well I didn't really love him. But slowly we did rebuild it, even as she came out from under Gary's thumb to the point that she now couldn't care less what he says to her. She's apologized to me over the years and asked me to forgive her for being so weak. She says she was just so afraid of growing old alone. At the time she rationalized it as "tough love," but she says that if she could go back and do it all over again, she would never let him change the locks on me.

The angels were right about another thing, when they said that my mother and I would always have this special connection with each other—truly a spiritual connection that goes beyond anything you can explain. The day I found out I was pregnant with my daughter, the phone rang just as I was walking in the door from my doctor's office, and it was my mom. "Elissa," she said, "I had a dream last night that you were pregnant, and it's a girl!" I hadn't told her I suspected it or even that I was going to the doctor—she just knew. Another night she called me with a darker vision. She said, "I just had a bad premonition of two guys trying to grab you in their car, to hurt you." She was so frightened that she was crying. "If anyone ever stops their car to try to lure you into it," she said, "you must run away!" "You know I would never get into a strange car with anyone," I said, "but don't worry, I'll be careful." The very next afternoon I was jogging along a busy road when a red Camaro pulled up alongside me, stinking of marijuana, with two very juvenile-delinquent-looking guys in it. And they told me to get in the car with them! Just as the guy in the passenger seat started to open his door to try and pull me in, I was reminded of my mother's warning, and I started running as fast as I could away from the car, screaming, "Help!" at the top of my lungs! When I turned around to see where the guy was, to my relief I saw that he'd gotten back in the car and they were driving away. Thanks to my mother's premonition, my instinct to protect myself was quicker than their impulse to grab me, and I was able to run safely away from the danger my mother had foreseen.

As far as our relationship being no bed of roses, we most definitely do have our ups and downs, where one minute she'll drive me crazy and the next we're best friends! But I could not imagine my life without her in it. Especially now that she is getting on in her years, I try to be more patient with her and come from a place that's filled strictly with love and understanding for her.

Well, the angels told me that if I chose to come back to my life, I would have to fight hard to get what I wanted. I am proud to say that I am fighting hard now to go down the right path, one that is filled with light and love, no more darkness. Sometimes you truly need to hit rock bottom before you can pull yourself out of that hole and climb your way up the steepest mountain. Because once you get to the top of it, honey, there is no going back down, and you will know you can conquer anything in this world.

Chapter 13

The Reunion

After I separated from my husband, I felt like another huge weight had been lifted off my shoulders. Now I was a free woman, able to come and go and do as I pleased, no longer trapped within my own prison. I have always believed in the institution of marriage, but only when it is with the right person. Unfortunately, mine was with the wrong one! Now that I was older and wiser, I made a vow to *myself* that I wasn't going to get it wrong again. My husband and I were not legally separated; in fact, we were still living under the same roof. But our house was so big that we were living in separate wings, living completely separate lives. That was good enough for me for the time being, until I could find a divorce attorney I was comfortable with and confident in to handle my case.

My husband wasn't happy about my decision to leave him, so I figured it was better to ease him into it gradually, so as not to rock the boat any further. I tried to stay as civil with him as I possibly could, for my daughter's sake. By this time I'd already had my flashback to heaven and remembered more of my purpose: that I was God's messenger here on earth. I actually told that to my husband, and I said that if I were him, I wouldn't mess with God's messenger anymore.

Now, my husband was not too spiritual, but he was somewhat religious, and he did believe in God. When I first met him, his father had recently died, and he had prayed to God and his father in heaven to send him an angel. Sure enough, he met me that night—so you can be sure he did believe I was "heaven-sent"! I knew he had regrets about how he had treated me; he actually said that if he could take it all back, he would. I told him it was way too late for that.

At the same time, I was excited about the prospect of a whole new life, one that I knew would be filled with only light and love. I had been in the dark for far too long. I knew in my heart of hearts that God had a better plan for me. And it was a time of self-discovery. I had gotten married when I was twenty-six years old. Now that I was forty-three, I knew much better who I was, where I was going in life, and the kind of person I wanted to share my passion and purpose in life with. It had to be a mature, special, spiritual man. No more mama's boys need apply! I had been in a dysfunctional marriage for so long that I'd almost forgotten what a healthy, happy relationship could be like. Nevertheless, I was determined to find out!

Over the years, there were always times when my thoughts would turn to my first love, Ron. I figured he must be married by now, with children. Even so, I found myself thinking about him now that I was more free. I wondered if, had we met each other when we were a little bit older, things would have turned out differently between us. I tried to put him out of my head, but for some reason he kept coming back, and one day I found myself googling him on the computer. Then I looked him up on Facebook, not really expecting to find him there. To my surprise, there he was, staring me right in the face—Ron, my Ron! His picture was exactly the way I remembered him, and a flood of memories came rushing back to me—the whole feeling of that time we had shared.

Ron was married, as I'd thought, and living in California. I found his website, and he had his e-mail address posted there. I really wanted to get in touch with him, just for old times' sake if nothing else. I said to myself, *What's the worst that could happen?* That he wouldn't write me back. And that was a chance I was willing to take. So I wrote a nice little e-mail. I tried to keep it light: *Hey, Ron, remember me? A blast from your past!* Then I went on to say that I'd come across him on Facebook and wanted to see how life had been treating him all these years. I kept my finger poised over the Send button for a minute, then took a deep breath and pressed. And off it went, the computer screen confirmed: *Your message has been sent.*

Gulp! Okay, I told myself, nothing ventured, nothing gained. I tried to reassure myself that I was just getting in touch with an old friend. Never mind that he might have been the love of my life! I had e-mailed him on a Friday, then gone away for the weekend. When I came home and checked my e-mail on Monday morning, I gasped to see that I had a message from him. For a moment I stared at it in disbelief—it just made me so happy to see his name in my mailbox. Then I opened up his message and was even happier to see how happy he was to hear from me!

I was happier still, I admit, when I read that he was separated from his wife, in a situation much like mine, living in the same house but in separate bedrooms, separate lives. He told me a little more about his life, writing that he had three daughters and was in the finance business. Then he told me something I couldn't believe: he said he still had the modeling slide of me that I'd given him, right in his bass guitar case, the slide I had given him when we first met at Soaps Alive twenty-eight years before.

Naturally, I had to write back, and the first thing I told him was that I still had his pictures too—the Polaroids he'd given me of him and his band the night we met. Only I kept them in my keepsake box, where I keep only my most cherished memories. I told him how meaningful they still were to me.

After that I wanted to write him something funny, so I decided to tell him about my short and not-so-brilliant career as a flight attendant, after modeling and before meeting Freddy. Not surprising that I was not a great success, considering I'm afraid of heights. I told Ron how, when the plane hit turbulence, I yelled for the passengers to assume crash positions, that the plane was going down! I told him how I always thought we were going to die, and it was the passengers who wound up comforting *me*, reassuring me that the plane was not in fact going down and that we were all going to live. I told him they really could have made a comedy out of the flight attendant that I was! Fortunately, I resigned from that job and told them I thought it would be best for everyone all around if I found a new career, with my two feet on the ground. For the record, I told Ron, I never joined the mile-high club either, though there were a couple of pilots who did try and persuade me! To this day, I can't understand why they were sad to see me go. Maybe I provided a little comic relief in the air?

Well, one thing led to another with Ron and me, and we kept exchanging e-mails. He asked me to send him a recent photo of myself, and when I did, he wrote back *What a hot mama!* I couldn't help myself—I responded, *Hot for you babe!*

Then I started to receive signs about him. The first one came one morning while I was in the shower: something told me to get out of the shower immediately and go look Ron up on Facebook, that there would be a new picture of him there. You know I always pay attention to signs! So I jumped out of the shower and ran to my computer, still dripping wet, and sure enough, there was a new photo of Ron on his Facebook page. He had replaced his old profile picture with one just taken of him recently. I couldn't believe how different he looked, so grown-up. He was a handsome, mature man now. I printed out the picture and put it in my keepsake box along with the other pictures I had of him from years before. And sure enough, the next day when I checked his Facebook page again, not only was the picture no longer there, the page wasn't there at all. It no longer existed. Now I knew why I'd received that sign to jump out of the shower and check when I did—because that picture was meant for me! Turned out that Ron did post the new picture for me, but then for business reasons he decided it would be better if he weren't on Facebook anymore. Now I was certain that this was another sign: that Ron and I should have a twenty-five-year reunion with each other, since it had been twenty-five years since our last date. When I mentioned it to him, he agreed that we definitely should. He told me that his company sometimes flew him to New York on business, and that the next time he was in the city he would come out to see me on Long Island.

That day came on September 22, 2011. The morning of our twenty-five-year reunion, I excitedly got my daughter off to school on the school bus, then started getting ready in sweet anticipation of the big moment. I wasn't the slightest bit nervous, just excited! I did my hair and makeup the best I could, and I put on a black cotton miniskirt with a black tank top. It was about 75 degrees out that day, so I figured he would appreciate seeing a bit of skin! At least my skin looked normal this time.

We had actually planned to meet in July, and I felt that I was too pale for summer, because I stay out of the sun after having had skin cancer a long time ago. So I did a fake tan. A week before our planned reunion, I applied sunless tanning cream to my skin every day. The result was a nice tan, along with bright orange palms. No one told me it would be best to apply the tanning cream with gloves on! I was almost relieved when Ron missed the train and couldn't meet me. He apologized over and over, promising that we would have our reunion the next time he came to New York. It had taken two weeks for those darned orange palms to fade, so this time I decided, no fake tan.

Now that summer had ended, I decided au naturel was best. I completed my outfit with a leopard-print belt, leopard heels, and a big faux fur leopard bag. I observed myself in the mirror and thought I looked pretty chic! That was my goal, to look attractive, but not in a trampy way. I put on my favorite perfume, Coco by Chanel, and headed out the door to the train station once again. Once again the train he was supposed to be on came and went without him on it. *Oh, no,* I thought to myself, *This can't be happening again. Don't tell me he missed this train too!* Then I checked my cell phone, and there was a message from him saying he'd accidentally gotten off at the wrong stop. He was catching the next train and would be there in twenty minutes. I smiled to myself at how sexy his voice sounded — still like him, but deeper, more mature. When the next train pulled into the station, it all happened so fast, it was like a scene out of the movies. The train door opens, and there he is, standing right in front of me, as if no time had passed at all. We threw our arms around each other as I squealed, "Ron! I don't believe it, it's so good to see you, it's been so long." He was just as tall, dark, and handsome as I remembered him, and his embrace was just as warm.

We got in my car and drove to the Huntington Hilton as we'd planned. Now, don't go getting any ideas! Nothing happened, although I sort of wished it did! Ron had only three hours, as he was scheduled to fly back to California that evening, so we just had time to eat lunch there and catch up with each other. I have to tell you, we barely came up for air! We talked the whole three hours, barely stopping to eat our food. I told him all about my near-death experience, which I'd never told him before, and he was fascinated. Then he told me that the last time we spoke, when he was moving to Chicago, he was just closing the door behind him when the phone rang and he ran back in the house to get it — and it was me! I got chills at that, and he said that he felt it was a sign too. Remember, we hadn't spoken in three years at that point. "I think it meant I was trying to stop you from moving," I said. "But if you had to leave, to remember me, and to come back for me one day." "I think it's a sign too," he said, "that I got off the train right at the door where you were standing. On that whole long train, what are the odds of that?"

Then I told him something else that had recently happened to me, just a very short time after he and I reconnected. I was at a party where they had a palm reader, and what she said blew me away. She said, "You were only in love two times in your life. The first one" — which was Ron — "you were very young, and you were separated for a long time, only to be brought back together again."

There was one other sign I couldn't ignore. When my grandmother was on her deathbed, I had asked her if she would send me my soul mate from heaven. She said, "I will if I can." Then she said I would know that she did, if he expressed kindness to me. And as we talked about our lives that day, at one point Ron turned to me. "Are you looking for kindness?" he asked me. "Is that all you want — someone to be kind to you?" I knew my grandmother was giving me a sign when he said that, that she did send my soul mate! The spark had been there since the moment we saw each other at the station. As we were leaving the restaurant, his bare arm brushed against mine, and the touch of his skin sent tiny shivers up and down my spine. When we got to the car, I was disappointed when he said he had to call his office — until he reached for me while he was still on the phone and held me close against him while he talked. As I drove back to the station with one hand on the wheel, he held my free hand and caressed it gently. I had lost my virginity to Ron when I was sixteen, and now that I was separated, I told him I was his born-again virgin and would save myself for him as long as I had to. That made him laugh. "Hopefully it won't be too long," he said.

When we pulled into the station, the train was already there, and we ended our beautiful reunion hastily, with one sweet kiss — and what a kiss it was! I could feel the hunger inside of him, and I'm sure he felt mine too. This was my first love, my only love, and knowing he had to leave me once again brought tears to my eyes. Only this time I was certain that when the time was right we really would be together, and we wouldn't have to part again. I felt sure that my guardian angels in heaven were making plans to seal the deal this time!

Chapter 14

Heaven Is a Place on Earth

After my wonderful day with Ron, something else wonderful started to happen. I started to receive pennies from heaven! I wondered if this was God's way of blessing our reunion? Or was it His way of letting me know that He was ready—or rather I was ready—to have the last piece of the puzzle put in place for me? Whatever it meant, it was a beautiful sign to me. Wherever I went, it seemed, there would be a heads-up penny that seemed to have appeared out of nowhere. Whether I was on line at the supermarket, or at the ice-cream parlor with my daughter, or even at the library, I would look down and there would be a penny, heads up, next to my foot. I would smile, pick it up, and say to my daughter, "Look, another penny from heaven!" One day, when I did this, her eyes welled up with tears. "Why can't the angels send me pennies from heaven too?"

Not long after, we were at the library again. I had already received my penny when I heard my daughter yell out from across the room—which I know the librarian didn't appreciate, as you're supposed to keep your voice down in a library! But my daughter was ecstatic because someone had sent her a penny from heaven too. I walked across the floor to where she and her friend were building something out of blocks. "Look, Mom," she said, and pointed to a penny right next to her foot, heads up. "See, honey," I exclaimed, "you got a special penny too!" She was beaming as she placed her penny from heaven in her jeans pocket. When we got home, it went straight under her pillow, where she keeps it for good luck. I place all of mine in a jar, as there are just too many of them to tuck under my pillow!

I did wonder what all these pennies were adding up to—but I didn't have to wonder for long, because God decided to reveal it to me on my forty-fifth birthday. I can't think of a greater birthday present than that! I woke up once again in the wee hours on the morning of my birthday, just as I did that night two years before. Once again, my whole near-death experience unfolded before my eyes, as if it were happening again. Only this time I didn't just remember that I was sent back as a messenger from God—I remembered *why*.

Like a bolt of lightning would strike someone, or a roll of thunder, it came crashing back to me and I remembered it all. There in heaven, He told me that I was hand-selected to be a special angel here on earth, to do His spiritual work in the world. I was the angel He was sending back to spread his message of light and love to the world, to try to make this world a better place to live in.

Wow! I thought to myself. No wonder He'd waited all these years to reveal that to me. I surely wouldn't have been able to handle such a big responsibility as a teenager, but now, as a middle-aged woman, it was nice to know I was also a middle-aged angel! I said a prayer to God to thank Him for finally revealing my whole purpose to me. I promised that, now that I knew what it was, I would take it very seriously and do all that I could to fulfill my purpose for Him. I thanked Him for my lovely birthday gift of angel wings. While they may have been invisible to everyone here on earth, including me, it touched me to know that God saw them on me all those years. And I vowed to dedicate the rest of my life to spreading the wisdom of light and love, peace and purpose, to make the earth a better place— to help make heaven a place on earth.

When I got out of bed later that morning, sure enough, as I went to put on my slippers, there was a shiny penny heads up in the left one. Later on that day, I took out my journal to write in it; there is a little angel on the cover, and there was a penny on top of the angel—heads up.

How do you make heaven a place on earth? You don't do it

all at once! But if everyone was a little bit kinder to everyone else each day, if everyone did a good deed every day or at least as much as they could, then that light and love would be bound to spread. If we all opened up our hearts and sent God's love out not just to our loved ones, but to everyone everywhere, we'd start a ripple effect that would be felt the whole world over. It could be as simple as holding a door open, or giving money to your favorite charity, or giving a homeless person money to buy lunch that day, or going to your local animal shelter and adopting a precious pet so in need of a loving home. To know that one life has breathed easier because of you—that is purpose, and that is love.

I must tell you a sign I received at the very moment I was writing that sentence about adopting a pet from a shelter. As I sat there at the computer in the library, a woman walked up to my daughter, who was sitting next to me, and the woman was holding a beautiful puppy that she had just adopted from her own local shelter that day! She asked my daughter if she could help her pick out a name for her new puppy. How is that for a sign? My daughter, happy to oblige, said, "What about Lucky?" To which the kind woman responded, "Lucky it is!"

Remember, there are no coincidences; this was definitely purpose and energy in motion! I received another beautiful sign from my beloved miniature dachshund, Frankie, on the one-year anniversary of the day he went to heaven. I called my mom on my cell phone from my car, and as I was dialing her number, before the call went through—I had it on speaker—a man's voice said, "Frankie." "Did you hear that?" I said to my daughter. "Yes," she said. "What did they say?" "Frankie!" If my daughter hadn't been sitting right next to me and confirmed what I heard, I might have questioned it myself. We had no idea who it was; it wasn't anyone on my mom's end of the line, because when she answered she said she was the only one home. I knew it was a sweet sign, a way for my little Frankie to let me know that he was happy in heaven, yet still with me spiritually. It also confirmed to me how intertwined heaven and earth really are, and how, the more positive energy you put out into the universe, the more it will come back to you in the most profound ways.

It especially warms my heart when I see children doing good deeds. I recently heard of a story where a group of fourth graders started a dog-walking business to help their teacher, whose daughter had spinal muscular atrophy and needed a service dog. The dog cost $5,000, and the teacher couldn't afford it, so the kids in the class raised the money she needed, and the teacher's daughter now has the service dog she needs so badly, thanks to the kindness of these wonderful kids. When children do this kind of good, it shows that they can live their lives with purpose and divine awareness too, and how rewarding it is for their souls.

There are plenty of opportunities to send out love every day just by helping people in simple ways—and don't forget about helping animals, which I sometimes think I specialize in! One day I was leaving the house of a friend who lives next to a nature preserve—which is a fancier term for the woods!—when a man in a convertible drove by me, and I could see he was in distress. He asked me if I'd seen an Alaskan malamute, which I knew was a dog that looked like a Siberian husky. "No," I said, "why?" And he explained that his dog had run away from him, and had been spotted going in and out of the woods where we were for the past two months. "I've been coming to these woods every single day," he told me, "and I just cannot catch him." Every time he called the dog's name, the dog took off running in the other direction. He left out food and water for him, and even set out a large Havahart (humane) trap in hope of finding the dog in it, but the dog was never there. "Winter is coming," he said, and he started to cry. "I'm afraid he won't last if I don't catch him soon."

Now, being the extreme dog lover that I am, and having saved many dogs from kill shelters by finding them good homes before they are put down, I felt so much sympathy for this man. I put my hand on his shoulder and said, "Go in the woods now. I'll pray to God that you come out with him this time." And as I was touching his shoulder, I felt this energy go from me to him. "Why should this time be different?" he said sadly. But he got out of his car and set off on foot into the woods, while I channeled all of my energy into praying to God that the dog should come to him this time. Not two minutes later I heard screaming from the woods. "Oh my God, I have him!" Then I saw the man coming out of the woods carrying this huge dog, and the dog was licking him all over his face.

"You don't understand," he said to me, trying to catch his breath, "I have been coming to these woods every day for the past *two months*. And every time I spotted him he just ran farther away. After you touched me and prayed for me, my dog came running into my arms." He looked at me closely. "I know that I was just touched by an angel," he said. I just smiled and patted his dog. I said, "Maybe you were."

I'm often asked the question, "Are you religious?" As you well might want to ask someone who has spent time in heaven! "No," I always say. "I'm spiritual." We are all God's children, all of us highly spiritual beings, so pure spirituality is really the only true "religion" there is. Even though I was born and raised Jewish, I must admit that I don't follow the Jewish religion, simply because I don't agree with it—or with any other religion, for that matter. Contrary to what a lot of people seem to think, converting people to your religion, whatever that happens to be, isn't the way to bring heaven to earth. I do feel it's part of my mission as God's messenger to tell people the truth about God Himself.

I was talking with the mother of one of Raphaela's classmates and it came up in our conversation that she didn't believe in

God at all—she called herself an atheist. I felt like shaking her and saying, "How can you not believe in God??" Instead, I just told her about my near-death experience, which I think is the strongest way I have of reaching people (and that's why you're reading this book!). When I got to the part about meeting God, I saw her mouth drop open. Then I said to her, "Who the heck do you think created you? Or your children? Or"—because she was pregnant—"the one that's growing inside of you now? Or the whole world? We didn't just come out of thin air, you know!" "I don't have the answer to that," she said. "Well, I do," I replied. "It is God who created everyone and everything." Not that I expected to change her mind right then, but at the end of our conversation, she did thank me for sharing my experience with her. She said I definitely gave her something to think about!

The truth is, the way the world is today is not the way it's supposed to be. God doesn't want to see blood shed, especially in senseless acts of violence. It breaks His heart when some dark soul brings about a tragedy that could have been prevented. God has the power to stop these things, but He won't, because that's why He created the world and its creatures. It's up to us to work it out among ourselves.

It is always easier to take the wrong way out, but the road less traveled is always the right path to be on. It may be more challenging, but in the end it is the most rewarding too, as well as the most enlightening. Rome wasn't built in a day, and neither is your life. It is an endless work in progress, a slow, gradual learning process. I promise you that if you live your life with integrity and don't hurt others along the way, each baby step will turn into bigger steps, and those will turn into giant leap steps! And before you know it, you will get there.

I'm here to tell you that everyone, including me, struggles on a daily basis to get it right, and I wouldn't have it any other way. Because when I do make those giant leap strides, it is the greatest feeling in the world! And that is when I realize that the road less traveled is the only one to take—the only road that will lead us all to the place where we all need to be. A place that is filled with light, where there is no room for darkness, or crimes of passion, or senseless evil acts. A place where God wants us all to be, while He sits up on His throne watching over all of us, praying that one day we will make heaven a place on earth.

Chapter 15

At the Throne of God

When I tell people about my experience in heaven, they often say to me, "You should write a book!" This is that book. And my prayer is that it may inspire everyone who reads it to help heal the world's suffering and bring heaven to earth as God intended.

Some time ago, I had started writing letters to families who'd lost loved ones in tragic ways, to try and ease their pain. I wrote to the mother who lost her children in the Christmas fire, and I wrote to a woman who lived in Long Beach, not far from me, when she lost her seven-year-old daughter, Katie, in a horrifying car accident that made national news. I would tell them all about my near-death experience and how beautiful heaven was, and I would tell them they mustn't blame themselves for what happened, because everything is already written in the book—there was nothing they could have done to prevent it. I thought that this would be comforting to people in their time of grief, and I knew that if it helped them to shed one less tear, it was worth my writing to them. And sometimes I really did know that it helped them: when I saw Katie's mom at the local library, attending a Mommy & Me class with her two-year-old son, though she was badly scarred from her own injuries in the crash and she still looked tremendously sad, she told me she'd found comfort in my words.

That was when I knew that it wasn't enough to write a couple of letters. That the time had come to write this book. God knew I was going to write this book long before I did. After all, this book was written in the book! But even when I felt the time had come to write it, I wasn't sure exactly how I would write it or even what I would say. I only knew that by putting all my faith and trust in God, I was putting it in His hands. I am His messenger, but He is my voice, coming through me every second of my life, guiding me where he wants to go. He had promised that the reason He was sending me back—the final piece of my near-death experience—would be revealed to me when the time was right, and it was.

I remembered it just as I was sitting down to write! Remember earlier when I said God showed me one more thing before he sent me back from heaven? First he took me up a staircase to a platform where, perched high up, His throne sat—a chair fit for a king, or in this case, God! It was very ornate, like something you'd see in the home of royalty, only there were no fancy trappings around it, as this was heaven, not a palace. God's throne overlooked a canyon, and in the canyon, where only God could see it, was the world.

Sitting high up there, God watched over it all. He raised His hand and pointed, and when I looked, suddenly I could see the world too. And just like when the angels had shown me my funeral, I started to recognize people, only this time it wasn't my grieving family; it was me! I saw myself as a grown woman, and I realized that God was showing me a glimpse of what my future would be. What I didn't realize—what I wouldn't realize until many years later—was that it was my future after writing this book, my future as a messenger spreading God's love on earth.

And what a future it was! I saw this grown-up version of me being whisked in a limousine from one talk show to another, sitting in front of the cameras, everyone wanting to meet me, everyone wanting to talk to me. I was at the center of a media frenzy! And naturally, being a teenager, I was very excited to see this. I turned around and saw that God was watching me while I watched my life.

"I am granting you your wish for fame," He said, "but not for the reason that you think." I could only assume it was because I was going to make it big as a supermodel, which was my dream.

But God had something different in mind. "Your wish is being granted for a much more important reason," He told me. "To tell people what I'm telling you, so they can be healed."

Then God told me to spread the message all over the world that He did not create any of us to hurt any of His creation. He doesn't want us to harm animals or kill each other. He doesn't want us to take our own lives. What he *does* want to see are acts of kindness in the world: the rich helping the poor, the young helping the old, the stronger helping the weaker ones, those who are well helping those who are sick, and all of it arising from love, which, as we know, can move mountains.

Life is a mystery, a rare and precious gift, and God has a special plan and purpose for each and every single one of us. Even as we are all on our own individual, unique journeys through our lives, we all share one thing in common, and that is God's love. We all share that common thread. We all breathe the same air, and our hearts all share the same beat; there is God inside all of us. He created all of us, and God doesn't make any mistakes, even though we do! When *you* make a mistake, God wants you to learn a lesson from it. When you fall down in life, He wants you to pick yourself up, dust yourself off, and carry on. When things don't go the way you hoped, it's not because God is punishing you; it's simply because it wasn't meant to be, and one day you will see the meaning in it. And when you suffer a major loss or have any kind of pain or suffering in your life, it's because your soul is in the process of experiencing real spiritual growth.

God gives, and He takes, but always with a silver lining behind each cloud. Pray to God every day, because the power of prayer is so great. God hears every prayer that He receives from every person, and He listens! Pray to him and He will always guide you down the path you're meant to be on. When you lose your way, God is only a prayer away. I'll admit that when I am feeling a little bit down, the constant reminder to myself that

God chose me to do His work here does lift my spirits. But in all honesty I prefer to think of myself as that same fourteen-year-old girl I was before I had my near-death experience, just a little bit more spiritual, with a couple more wrinkles!

I do know some things now that I didn't know when I was fourteen. I have learned that in a sense, life truly is about letting go, not holding on. I've learned that sometimes less really is more, since eventually we have to leave it all behind. The only things we get to hold onto are spiritual, not material, so how much do we really need to acquire in this lifetime? How big a house do you really need to live in, how many cars do you need to drive? Often the things with no price tag on them are the most precious.

Give your children an extra hug and kiss when you tuck them into bed at night. Take your dog for a run on the beach while you listen to the waves crashing on the sand. Never take a single moment for granted, and do unto others as you would have done to you. Laugh your loudest, love with all your heart, dance along the moonlight. Thank God each and every day for all the precious gifts in your life—and for every miracle, as a miracle is God at work.

Thank you for taking this journey with me this far. I sincerely hope I have been able to answer some questions for those of you who are searching for God and a deeper meaning in your lives. And for those of you who are already close to God, it is my wish that you have been brought closer to Him than ever.

It is with the deepest gratitude to God that I say He made it possible for me to write when He appointed me His personal messenger. I hope and pray that God and my guardian angels are proud of God's work that I am doing here on earth. I hope they are giving me a high-five sign, along with Frank Sinatra smiling down on me, crooning that, "I did it my way!" And I wish you all God's light and love always. May God bless all of us.

Part III

Twin Flames

Chapter 16

Prince Charming

I believe in fairy tales and true love. As well as happily ever after. Every girl dreams of her knight in shining armor galloping up on a white horse, and sweeping her off her feet. Then, riding off into the sunset together. At the tender age of sweet sixteen—I had an encounter with my Prince Charming. It was more of a vision, as I saw a picture of him.

Being that I was in the modeling industry, I came across male models all the time. I worked with them, and even dated some of them. But, none of them ever caught my eye the way that this one particular male model did. I just happened to be looking through one of the top modeling agencies' books. It was Zoli, a top NYC modeling agency. Naturally, I was going through the men's modeling division, and thought they were all very handsome. But, that was about all, until one of them caught my eye. And, I had this spiritual awakening that I cannot even fully explain even to this day. I only know that I exclaimed out loud—He is my Prince Charming! I am going to meet him one day!

Naturally my next thought was: yeah sure, Elissa, in your dreams! But, hey you can't blame a girl for dreaming, right? And, after all—isn't that what fairy tales are made up of? So, why burst my bubble. I truly felt in my heart that one day my Prince Charming and I would meet, fall in love, and live happily ever after. His name was Todd Irvin, and he was very handsome. I was absolutely drawn to him like a magnet. I was mesmerized by his blue eyes, and felt this spiritual connection to him. Every time I would turn the page to look at the rest of the male models, I kept going back to Todd. Something kept drawing me back to him.

Call it fate, intuition, or destiny but it was at that moment I knew: someday and some way our paths would cross. Of that I was sure of... I just didn't know that it was going to take thirty-four years to do so!

Chapter 17

Fairy Tales Do Come True

My fairy tale began thirty-four years after I first laid eyes on my Prince Charming—Todd Irvin's picture in his modeling agency's book. I declared when I saw his photo, and stared into the beautiful, penetrating blue eyes of his—that he was my Prince Charming! The man I was destined to be with one day.

It all started on Valentine's Day, February 14, 2017. I woke up that morning, feeling very unfulfilled. I knew my love life was going nowhere. I was still separated from my husband, and heading for divorce. And, what seemed like such a promising relationship with Ron was practically all but nonexistent now.

Since our reunion back in 2011, I had not seen him again. We kept in touch from time to time, by the occasional e-mails. And, that may have been good enough for him, but it certainly wasn't enough for me. My heart longed for so much more than that, and it was on Valentine's Day that I finally came to my senses. And decided—if you love something set it free, if it comes back to you it's yours—if it doesn't, it never was. I knew in my heart that Ron wasn't the right man for me after all—and that it was time to set him free. And, that was exactly what I did on Valentine's Day—set him free! I let go of any romantic feelings I had for him, so that my heart was free now to find my true love, and everlasting happiness. I had never had a healthy, happy loving relationship with a man before in my life. Starting with an emotionally cold, and distant father. My heart longed for a kind, loving sensitive man who would be everything that my father was not.

And, as I was meditating that Valentine's Day morning—I had a vision of Todd Irvin! And a voice inside me said: Todd is that kind, sensitive, and loving man you've been searching for your whole life! Then that same voice inside me said: get up, and google him on your computer. What are you waiting for, you fool! Go after your Prince Charming—it's only been thirty-four years!

I ran to my computer, not even expecting to find any information on him. After all, thirty-four years is a long time! Who knows where he could be now? To my surprise, he was in California. I laughed to myself—what was it with California? Ron was in California, now Todd too! *Oh boy,* I thought to myself—*here we go again!*

I learned that Todd was now a therapist in Santa Monica, California, and he was now sixty-two years old. He was twelve and a half years older than me, which suited me just fine. As I was ready for a relationship with a mature man. What I did not know was whether he was married, or not. Heck, for all I knew he could even be gay! A thought I immediately dismissed. I told myself that yes, some men were gay in the modeling industry. But that, God willing, Todd was not. And that I was just going to have to take a blind spiritual leap of faith, and pray for the best.

That's when I saw Todd's e-mail address on his therapy website, and I decided: dare I e-mail him? I knew it was a bold move, after all—he'd have no idea even who I was, other than a former model myself. But I thought to myself: it is Valentine's Day. So, perhaps it would be a cute gesture to send him a sweet Valentine's Day poem. I brought out the poet in me, and wrote: "Dear Todd, Roses are red, violets are blue, since I was sweet 16, I've had a crush on you. Will you be my Valentine?" Then I said: "RSVP by midnight tonight." I went on to say: "Like you I am a former model," and included an old modeling photo of myself, as well as a recent photo. I figured if he saw I was a model like he was, he would see we shared that common thread with each other. That I wasn't just anyone coming out of left field.

I had butterflies in my stomach when I sent the e-mail. My

heart started to race, and I thought — *OMG, Elissa, I can't believe I just did that!* Then I went about my day not expecting to hear from him at all.

Well I did! But, not until the next morning, at least that was what I thought. Because, I stopped checking my e-mail on Valentine's Day at 10:00pm. And, with the three-hour time difference from NY to California, Todd had actually e-mailed me back on Valentine's Day, as I had told him to RSVP by midnight. He wrote me back at 10:12pm California time which was 1:12am New York time. So, technically he made the deadline, as it was before midnight his time. But, I had already gone to bed 10:00pm my time, with a heavy heart thinking he didn't write me back. Who was I to think that Todd Irvin would respond to such a silly little e-mail? What kind of a dream world was I living in? It turns out, a very real one!

When I woke up the next morning to get my daughter off to school, I checked my e-mail, and could not believe my very eyes. Staring back at me was an e-mail from Todd! My Prince Charming does exist after all! I saw he e-mailed me back at 10:12pm. Just twelve minutes after I had gone to bed on Valentine's Day. and he wrote: "Elissa — I'm very flattered by your e-mail. Sorry that today was crazy, but I'll give you a call tomorrow. Happy Valentine's Day!!! Warmly, Todd." To say that my heart skipped a beat would be an understatement. Jumped out of my chest would be more like it! I was so happy, and so excited! As well as in major shock that he really responded to me. Which quickly eliminated the gay factor — thank you, dear God!

The wheels in my head started turning fast. My mind couldn't stop racing. After all, he did say he was going to call me today. OMG, what was I going to say to him? That you've been my Prince Charming since I was sixteen years old? And, that we are destined to be together! I decided to start off with a simple hello! And, just take it from there. Well I didn't have to worry about it too much, because he didn't call me until two months later! Which caught me totally by surprise. Because, I had thought for sure that he had gotten cold feet, and changed his mind. But, one Friday night, on April 14, 2017, the phone rang, and my daughter answered it. She yelled, a little too loud so that Todd could surely hear: "Mom, it's for you, it's that guy Todd you like!" Kids sure have a way with words! I grabbed the phone from her, and exclaimed with a little too much enthusiasm: "Is this the Todd Irvin?" and he laughed, and said: "It is!"

Just hearing his voice made me melt! I said to him: "What took you so long to call?" He apologized and said how busy he had been, and had been traveling as well. I immediately replied, "That's okay, better late than never!" Then, I went on to tell him that I would be spending most of the upcoming summer in California. And would love to get together while I'm out there. He said that he wanted to meet me too. And, took my cell phone number, and promised to call me when I was in California. It was Good Friday, and Easter was only two days away. So, we both wished each other a happy Easter, and hung up the phone. I thought to myself: only two more months until I meet my Prince, and that, fairy tales do come true!

Chapter 18

Meeting Todd

The plane took off on the morning of June 24, 2017. As I looked out of the window of the airplane—I found myself drifting off into the clouds. They looked so big, white, and fluffy—so dreamy. Which was exactly the way that I was feeling from the anticipation of finally getting to meet my Prince Charming. It made me literally feel like I was on cloud nine. To say my head was in the clouds was more like it! Part of me felt like I can't believe this is really happening, and the other part of me said: it's about time. After all, I was already fifty years old. Wasn't it time I met my soul mate already? Just call it intuition, I knew beyond the shadow of a doubt, that Todd was my soul mate. The man that I was destined to be with.

As the plane touched down at LAX Airport, my adrenaline was really pumping. I couldn't believe I was really in California, about to meet my prince! The plan was: I was going to text Todd to let him know I was here in California. I was totally exhausted from not having slept the night before due to total excitement! And, now I was also jet-lagged on top of my exhaustion. Therefore I decided I would get a good night sleep at the condo I was renting in Santa Monica. And, text Todd as soon as I woke up the next morning. Which was exactly what I did. I quickly sent Todd a text message to let him know I was in Santa Monica, and included my cell phone number. And, told him to call me to get together soon. I expected to hear back from him quickly.

Certainly within a day, or two. But, it actually was almost three weeks before he called me! And, during those three weeks, I was beginning to go stir crazy. I tried my best to keep busy, but my mind kept racing, thinking, Why isn't he calling or texting me? I knew there was no way I was leaving California without meeting him. Every night I went to sleep I would pray to God to please have Todd call me.

I even turned to my friend actor Ryan O'Neal for advice. I dialed his phone number, and Ryan answered on the third ring. I said: "Hey Ryan, it's Elissa." He said: "Would you believe I'm flat out on my back, for the past week, and bedridden from back surgery."

The poor thing just had major back surgery, and was in so much pain. I tried to cheer him up, then figured that since he was the star in the movie *Love Story* perhaps I could get some much-needed advice from him about Todd. And, sure enough I did! Ryan said, invite Todd over for a barbecue. And, I thought to myself—what a great idea! So, I thanked Ryan, and wished him well. What I have always loved about Ryan is his wonderful sense of humor! That man can always make me laugh! The poor man misses his soul mate, Farrah Fawcett. He told me he can't wait to be with her. And, I assured him when the time is right, he will be. He thanked me for making him feel better, and told me to call him again. That he liked talking to me because I was so easy to talk to.

When I got off the phone with Ryan, I decided it would be best to call Todd. I had texted Todd a sexy photo of me a week earlier and wrote, "Invitation for a romantic July 4th celebration. Let's set off some fireworks of our own—I'm sure there will be enough sparks between us!" I told him to RSVP by the 4th of July. Well, when July 4th came and went, I was starting to panic, and eat too many Krispy Kreme donuts! As I bit into my third Krispy Kreme I thought to myself enough is enough: I'm taking Ryan O'Neal's advice, and calling Todd. I left a message on his voicemail, and invited him over Sunday for a barbecue. I said: "Please let me know either way if you can make it," and hung up. Then, I waited for his reply.

It finally came the next evening while I was playing cards with my daughter. I got a text message from Todd saying, "I'm so sorry I've been having trouble with my phone, and I just got your messages now!" Then he went on to say: "I would love to come over for a barbecue tomorrow." I silently thanked Ryan O'Neal, and God!

Then my phone rang, and it was Todd! He kept apologizing over and over for the three-week delay. I said it's okay, as I knew we still had another month to spend together in California. He asked me what he could bring to the barbecue, and I quickly said yourself—thinking to myself, *I'll have you for dessert!* I gave him my address, and told him I would see him 6:00pm the next day. He said he was looking forward towards meeting me. He sounded so nice, and sincere. He said he was from Ohio, your typical laidback Midwestern boy.

I barely slept a wink that night as I was way too excited to meet him! I spent the whole next day cleaning the condo I was renting, and to my dismay the barbecue wasn't working! And I had invited Todd over for a barbecue! What was I going to do? Take him out to dinner, I decided! But, I figured I would tell him once he got here.

To say I counted down the hours, minutes, and seconds until six o'clock rolled around would be an understatement. I could not wait to meet him! Finally the time came, he texted me to say he was parking outside my condo. I texted back that I would meet him outside my complex in front of the gate as it was a gated complex. As I was walking down the three flights of steps, with each step my anticipation growing—I told myself, this is it, I'm finally meeting my Prince Charming! I waited my whole life for this very moment! I truly felt like Cinderella going to the ball. And, I knew "my life would never be the same again". And, sure enough I was right!

I didn't see Todd when I went to the gate where we were supposed to meet each other. So, I started to walk down the street, and still didn't see him. As I reached into my bag to pull out my cell phone to text "where are you?" I heard footsteps behind me.

Very much the same way I heard footsteps in heaven—only this time it wasn't God, but Todd! As I turned around there he was standing there with a bouquet of sunflowers for me in one hand, and a bottle of wine in the other hand.

I said: "Todd?" And he said: "Elissa?" Then, we both laughed, and hugged each other. And, I thanked him for the sunflowers. He didn't look anything like his modeling pictures. But, of course he wouldn't, as it was from thirty-five years ago! He was now sixty-two years old, and still very attractive for his age. I immediately felt at ease with him, so much in fact that I couldn't stop talking to him! And noticed that he couldn't stop talking to me either! We both seemed to have so much to say to each other!

We discovered that we had so much in common. He was someone I could genuinely be myself with. He was different from any other man I had ever been with. In fact, he was the first real man I had ever been with! I knew immediately there was a special connection between us.

The very first thing I told Todd about myself was that I was extremely spiritual. Being the incredibly smart man that he was he said: "Is it because you had a near-death experience?" My mouth dropped open and asked, "How did you know?" He laughed and said, "I figured that's why you're so spiritual!" I went on to tell him all about it, and he was fascinated by it. I asked him if he was spiritual. And he said he was, but would like to become even more so. Which, I told him, I will teach you more about it.

He told me he was a tai chi master. And, even studied with the great master—William CC Chen. Todd told me that tai chi is a form of meditation in motion. That it promotes serenity and peace. It is a noncompetitive martial art known for both its techniques and health benefits. It is the most effective exercise for health of mind, and body.

We also talked about our modeling days. I was just a working petite model. But Todd had been a top male model. A real superstar in his day! People used to come up to him, asking for his autograph. He was one of the highest paid top male models in the industry.

He worked with every female supermodel, as well as dated a number of them. He told me he slept with Elle Macpherson. And, I couldn't help but ask him if she earned the title of "the body", which he replied, "YES!" He also said that Brooke Shields was chasing after him for a while, and that his only regret was that he shouldn't have passed up Claudia Schiffer when she asked him out! He did have serious relationships with models Sophie Billard and Appollonia van Ravenstein, who he called "Apples". Todd worked with all of the top fashion designers, with Ralph Lauren being his favorite designer to work with. He told me, Ralph Lauren was the nicest man he had ever met.

Todd was also very fond of fashion photographer Bruce Weber, who Todd said was responsible for turning Todd into the international top male model that he became when Bruce shot the *GQ* magazine with Todd on the cover. Todd said that he and Bruce stayed friends throughout the years.

Todd traveled the world and did so many different fashion shoots on so many different exotic islands. It all sounded so glamorous to me. But, he confessed that he was more interested in helping people, and not just standing around posing in front of the camera looking good. He felt his true calling in life was to help others in need. And, I thought to myself: what an amazing man he is! As much as he didn't enjoy modeling he did enjoy the perks of it. Such as the fame and fortune—and the beautiful female models. Which was why he stayed a bachelor, and didn't get married until his forties.

He wound up marrying an Australian woman, Leeanne, who was a television producer. They had a beautiful daughter, named Ainslie, who Todd told me was the apple of his eye. Todd was separated like I was, and even more so, as they lived in separate houses.

When I told him the barbecue grill wasn't working, and I would take him out to dinner, he insisted on taking me out to dinner! So, I had a great idea. Let's just take a pizza pie back to my condo, and open up the bottle of red wine he brought, and sit out on my rooftop terrace. He agreed, and it was a perfect night. It was a warm beautiful July night, and we had a very romantic evening, gazing up at the stars. With me of course wishing upon one of them. And I'm sure you can guess what my wish was!

Todd must have read my mind, because right after I made my wish—he started to kiss me. And, all I could think was, *My prince is kissing me!* I had to pinch myself to make sure I wasn't dreaming! And then we fell into each other's arms, and really started to kiss passionately. The chemistry between us was electric! I could feel the sparks between us. I thought to myself: so this is what I'd been missing all these years! Having been in such a miserable, sexless, and loveless marriage, I closed my eyes, and enjoyed being desired by this wonderful man.

He started to take things a little bit further with me, but I told him that I'm not a one-night stand. But that the second night I just might! He laughed, and said he was glad to see I wasn't that type of girl. That most of the models he had dated always had sex on the first date. I told him I'm too spiritual to do that. And, he said that he totally respected me, and found it rather refreshing. It was getting late so we decided to call it a night. So, I walked him to the front door. As we kissed goodnight, and I was closing the door our eyes locked in an intimate embrace. It felt like time stood still in that moment. It seemed to hold the promise of what was yet to come for us. And I knew that I was already falling deeply for this man!

Chapter 19

Falling In Love

It truly was a perfect first date I had with Todd. He thought so too up until one tiny little mishap. About five minutes after Todd left, I received a text message from him. I thought how sweet he must be texting me to tell me he had a wonderful evening, and that he misses me already! But, to my dismay, it said: "My car isn't in the parking spot in the garage! One of the neighbors had it towed!" I texted back: "Oh no! Be down in a minute!"

I ran downstairs thinking: so much for our perfect first date! When I got to the indoor parking garage, I found Todd standing in the spot that his car should have been in! Luckily he was a good sport about it, because it was me who accidentally told him to park in the wrong spot! And, sure enough a neighbor did indeed have his car towed!

I drove him in my rental car to bail it out of tow truck prison! I thought to myself, *There goes our romance!* I seriously wondered if he'd ever want to see me again.

Fortunately, he did! When he called me the next day I joked around and said: "I bet that's one date you will never forget!" He laughed, and said absolutely! And, he said I'm ready for a second one! He asked me out for the following Saturday night. I figured I'd better make it up to him—so I wanted to look my prettiest for him. I went to a chic Beverly Hills salon, and got my hair cut and blown out. When Todd picked me up he immediately noticed it, and admired it.

I said to myself, "I'm not going to screw this date up," and had him park at the curb. I avoided the garage where Todd got his car towed like the plague. But, being that I do have a crazy sense of humor, I can't help but laugh about it every time I think of it. Todd probably didn't find it as amusing as I did! And, when I reimbursed him the $330 towing fee that I insisted on paying him back for—because it was totally my fault—I didn't find it so funny anymore either!

On our second date we went out to dinner to a lovely seafood restaurant. We chose to sit outside at a quaint picnic table. Todd and I had seafood, and he drank some beer. I can't hold my liquor so I only had a few sips of his beer. When we both swung our legs around the picnic bench to stand up, we both stumbled, and fell off of it! Needless to say, we both started cracking up, and laughed ourselves silly arm in arm while we strolled out onto the beach to take a walk along the ocean.

The sun was setting, and the sky was the most picturesque I have ever seen it. A mix of dazzling colors. I thought to myself if I didn't know any better, I may have thought I was dreaming! As if the second date could be any better than the first date—it was! As we strolled along the ocean, Todd turned to me, and took me in his arms and pulled me closer to him. We passionately embraced, while hearing the waves of the ocean gently brush our feet. And I felt like this is exactly where I should be. That I could feel something incredibly special taking place between the two of us. Our connection was undeniable. We truly enjoyed each other's company. So much in fact, that we were inseparable for the rest of the summer that I spent in California with Todd.

One night while I was laying in Todd's arms I said to him, "You have some sadness in you, don't you?" He said, "You can tell?" I said, "Yes, because of how intuitive I am." Then I immediately said, "Don't worry, I'll heal you." Todd exclaimed, "Where did you come from?" I replied, "God!" Todd then said, "You're my angel." And, from that moment on he always referred to me as "his angel". He said I was sent back from heaven to be his angel.

He started to truly open up to me and confide in me about the deepest parts of his life, and himself. He told me how he was carrying around enormous guilt that his oldest brother had committed suicide. Todd felt so guilty because his brother had called him just before he took his life. Todd heard the phone ringing but thought it was one of his clients calling. By this time Todd was now a licensed family and marital therapist, and he was tired from a long day at work. So, he decided not to answer the phone. Todd said it immediately rang again, and once again he ignored it, and went to sleep. The next morning when he woke up he found out that his brother had committed suicide, and that was him calling Todd just before he killed himself. Todd never forgave himself for not answering the phone. He felt like he could have talked him out of taking his own life. His brother and he were very close, and Todd carried that guilt around him for the longest time.

As Todd was telling me how he'll never forgive himself, I felt his brother's spirit enter the room. A warm breeze came upon me, but all the windows were shut. I knew it was his brother reaching out to Todd. I told Todd I had just made contact with his brother, and that he can talk to John, and tell him whatever he wanted to say. Todd said, "I'm so sorry, John, that I didn't take your two phone calls when you needed me the most. Please forgive me." Then John communicated to me that there was nothing Todd could have done to have prevented it from happening. That he was only calling him to say goodbye. I relayed that message to Todd, and Todd let out the biggest sigh of relief. And said: "I love you, John." Then, I told Todd that John said he loves Todd too. Then his brother's spirit left the room. Todd was so overcome with emotion that he started to cry, and thanked me and said: I really was his angel.

Todd also opened up to me about how sad he was that he didn't get to see his daughter as much as he would have liked to. That was the hardest part of his separation for him, with his daughter living with her mom. He loved his daughter so much, and not being able to see her every day or on certain holidays was rough on him. But when he did see her, he was so happy. I could see how much he loved her, because his eyes would light up every time he spoke of her. He told me how when she was little that she was truly daddy's little girl.

He constantly would tell me how I was the only bright spot in his life. I felt the same way about him too. I had just as much stress in my life too. Freddy was still abusive and disrespectful to me. Todd and I were each other's safe haven. As our relationship kept growing, we knew we were falling in love. Todd told me he loved me the night before I flew back to New York. I told him that I loved him too. So much in fact that I burst out into tears when the plane to NY took off. I did not want to leave him. It was the very last thing I had wanted to do. It took every fiber of my being not to get off that airplane, and run back straight into the arms of the man that I loved! I cried all the way back to New York. I had the most perfect summer with the most incredible man. I felt like I was leaving my heart behind in California. As soon I was leaving the plane, I knew I was a different woman. And, I thought to myself, *I am truly in love.* It had nothing to do with Todd Irvin the former famous model. I had fallen so deeply in love with this man's heart, and soul.

After the first time Todd made love to me, he held me in his arms and said, "We're kindred spirits." And I said: "Yes, my darling, we are." He would always tell me that he was intrigued by me; that he thought I had the most beautiful heart, and soul. He would say, "You're just a good-hearted person." One day, with tears in his eyes, he said, "You're the most beautiful woman that I ever met." I had never connected on this level with anyone before, and fell so in love with him. I would thank God every day for blessing me with him, and the special love that we shared. We had this magical spiritual connection. We connected on every level physically, mentally, emotionally, and spiritually. And, we were so excited that we had found each other, and knew that what we had was unique, and special.

Chapter 20

Soul Mates

Todd and I would burn up the phone lines from NY to California. We were the perfect example of how you can make a long distance relationship work. Because of our love for each other, we did it so effortlessly. Todd sometimes didn't finish with his last client until 9:00pm his time, which because of the three-hour time difference from NY to California was 12:00am my time. So, I used to get midnight phone calls from him all the time. When we couldn't be together in person, we were on the phone. My daughter was in school so I had to be here for her. As soon as school let out for the summer, I went back to California to be with Todd. Boy, how I would count down the months, weeks, days, minutes, and seconds until I was back in my Todd's arms once again. Sometimes I felt I would burst until we were back together again. But, being the wonderful therapist that he was, he was so good at communicating that our long conversations on the phone almost took the place of when we couldn't see each other.

The second summer out in California with him was very emotional for him. His brother Chris was selling their grandparents' island in Canada that Todd had spent every summer at when he was growing up. It was such a sentimental place for him, and he was devastated about the sale. He knew his parents who were no longer living would not have wanted that. Todd said they wanted it to be passed on as a family legacy from generation to generation. Todd was very close to his parents, especially his mother. He said I reminded him of his mother, and that his parents would have loved me. He said his mom's dream was to be a stewardess, and Todd knew that I had been a flight attendant. Although not a very good one, because of my fear of heights!

He said his mom and I had similar quirky personalities! Todd's brother Chris and he were at odds with each other over the sale of this island. In fact it had caused such a rift between them that they were barely on speaking terms. Todd was in tears the morning he was leaving to go to Canada to sell it. It had been in his family for almost a hundred years! I was still in California with him, and the night before he had to leave I gave him a "sending you healing thoughts" card. It said: "I hope you know you're in the prayers I offer day by day to thank God for the precious blessings life has brought my way. And at this time especially I'm asking in each prayer that God will heal and bless you and keep you in his care." Then I wrote in it, "My dearest Todd, I believe that God sent me to you just when you needed me most. And, that I promise you — even in your darkest hour there will be light. My light and love will always be with you! Love, your angel, Elissa." Todd said he loved my card, and brought it with him to Canada.

When he returned from Canada he was upset that the island where he spent every summer since he was a baby was no longer a part of his life. I held him in my arms, and comforted him. And told him that he should cherish all of the beautiful memories he had spent with his family at their island. I told him that maybe even one day we could buy it back! He loved that idea, and with a twinkle in his eyes he said, "I love you."

Our relationship continued to grow. We enjoyed each other's company so much that it didn't matter what we were doing. Even if we were just hanging out we were so happy being together. There were no awkward silences between us. We were truly each other's soul mates. We both agreed that a love like ours comes along once in a lifetime. I never knew love like this before, and it filled the deepest part of me. We would say that we were each other's better half, and that together we were whole and really completed each other.

Around this time, I wrote a reality television show called *The Cat Angel*. I was "The Cat Angel." The concept of it was that it was a reality *Touched by an Angel* show. About my near-death experience. How I died, went to heaven, and came back as an angel. To rescue cats in need of help. Todd and I chose to rescue only cats, because Todd's good friend Robert Dalrymple, who was a successful Hollywood producer, loves cats. Todd said Robert is obsessed with cats. He thought Robert would be interested in producing *The Cat Angel*. So, I wrote up a pitch for *The Cat Angel*, and Todd fine-tuned it. Because Todd once had a production company, he knew how to perfect the script I wrote before he presented it to Robert. Todd was excited that Robert loved it! He was very enthusiastic about it, and told Todd that we would pursue it further once he was done with a couple of other projects he had started already. I was proud of myself for creating a show that a Hollywood producer loved. And told Todd that he will be one of the executive producers on it. Everything seemed to be falling into place so perfectly for Todd and me. We both discussed getting divorced, and spending the rest of our lives together. We were the happiest we had ever been in a relationship. We were each other's best friend and soul mate. We never knew what was looming in the distance, but were about to find out!

Chapter 21

Endless Love

Love never dies... it is endless. I was about to find out just how very true that was. So far, I had two perfect summers with my Todd in California. Now I was enjoying my third summer with him. It was a sweet one because his best childhood friend was visiting him from Ohio too. They had been friends since kindergarten. So, it was lovely to meet such an old friend of Todd's. Todd was excited to take Dwight and me to see his new therapy office which he had recently moved to, in a bigger, better building.

I'm not sure why but as soon as I walked into Todd's office—I wanted to cry. I just couldn't shake this overwhelming feeling that was making me so overly emotional. When Todd sat down next to me on the couch, I didn't want him to leave me. I held his hand, and refused to let go. I suppose he thought I was being affectionate, but I knew that there was more to it than that. Something just was upsetting me, and yet I couldn't put my finger on what it was. But, I sat back and tried my very best to relax, and again for whatever reason, couldn't take my eyes off of Todd. I felt this rush of adrenaline, and surge of love for him. Again, I wanted to weep tears of emotion. I think it was because in that moment in his office, I have never loved him more than I did then and there. And, little did I know that would be the first and last time I would be in that office with him. As well as our last summer together.

It was almost as if Todd had a premonition too—because he kept talking about my near-death experience and asking me what heaven was really like. And usually it was the other way around, with me talking to him about heaven. I answered all of his questions, and he even asked me if it hurts when you die. I told him it does not hurt and it's just as natural as being born—just a different process.

The rest of our summer together was beautiful as always. When we were saying goodbye before I boarded the plane, I remember not taking my eyes off of him while he walked away. Something that I had never done before. I stood there, and waited until he was no longer in sight. With a heavy heart I boarded the plane. I was always sad to be leaving him. But, this time, my heart was heavier than usual. I tried to relax on the plane, but something was bothering me. This continued even when I arrived home in New York. I started waking up during the night with panic attacks. I had never had a panic attack in my life before! I had this bad feeling that I just couldn't shake.

The holidays were approaching, and usually I get into the holiday spirit. This time, I did not feel in a festive mood at all. In fact, my panic attacks were getting worse. I didn't want to worry Todd about them, so I didn't tell him. We rang in the New Year on the phone together. And, once again my panic attacks continued to wake me up at night.

Then, one night I had a dream: Todd came to me, and was hugging me goodbye. And letting me know that he loves me, and will always be with me spiritually. When I woke up from my dream that morning, I found out that my dear, sweet precious Todd had died.

I fell to my knees, and collapsed on the floor. I was in total shock, but was hysterically crying too. I was screaming, "Not my Todd, not Todd!" It was the worst pain I have ever been in. I was beyond heartbroken. I kept crying. I didn't even get to say goodbye to him. Then I realized my darling Todd had come to me in my dream and hugged me goodbye, just before I woke up to find out he had died. It was of some comfort knowing he loved me enough to come to me the way he did. He knew I would not have been able to bear his death had he not come to me in my dream to let me know he was still with me spiritually, and always will be.

Being as intuitive as I am—I asked Todd to let me know how he died and immediately I got a deep pain in my heart. It was a real throbbing pressure on my chest. Sure enough I found out that he had had a massive heart attack. And that he was found dead in his office!

I was in tremendous pain. I could barely eat or sleep. I had just lost the love of my life, my everything. The only thing keeping me going was I kept receiving signs from Todd all the time! I believe it is because of my near-death experience and my time spent in heaven that Todd and I are so spiritually connected. Todd even came to my mother in a dream, and she said he looked confused because he was looking for me!

The night he died, my television kept turning on and off! That has never happened before. Then the next night my heat shut off, and it was a cold January night. Normally without heat, I would be freezing. But, this time I wasn't cold at all. I knew my Todd was keeping me warm. When the man came to fix the problem the next day he said there was no explanation for why it happened! I knew it was my Todd!

A little while before Todd died he had taken my hands in his and looked me in the eye, and said if it is meant to be, it will be. That if he and I are destined to be together forever then we will be.

I was in so much pain after losing him that I said out loud to him, "I need a sign from you if it is meant to be, and we are soul mates. And you're waiting for me in heaven. Then give me a sign." When I woke up on the morning of his funeral, and looked out my patio door, I saw in the water two beautiful white swans gently floating together! When the swans were almost out of my sight, they both turned around towards me, their necks entwined, and their bills touched, kissing each other. I cried, "That's my sign from Todd!" That we are soul mates, and it is meant to be, and he is waiting for me in heaven!

Never before in the fourteen years that I have been living in my home have there ever been any swans in the water in my backyard. Only geese, or seagulls, but not any swans. That was the first and only time, on the morning of his funeral, there has ever been a swan. And that they were there just when I looked outside my patio door. That these two magnificent, beautiful swans were right before my very eyes, straight in front of me. There's no mistaking that was Todd's sign to me! I knew Todd sent the ethereal pair of swans to me to deliver a spiritual message to me.

Sure enough I found out that a pair of swans are the Twin Flames spirit animal and represent the eternal love of oneness between two beings. Twin Flames are one soul that was split into two bodies and share the same consciousness. They are very rare because they are sent here during their last lifetime when their soul is very advanced. And are sent here as a light worker by God to raise the vibration of love and energy throughout the world. Twin Flames are in the Bible, and Adam and Eve were Twin Flames.

I was so amazed to know that Todd and I were Twin Flames connected for all of eternity. That our soul has been together from the moment of creation, and will spend all of eternity together. And that it is actually my beloved Twin Flame Todd who finally revealed my whole purpose to me of why God sent me back to my life from heaven as his light worker to spread his light, love, and energy throughout the world!

Now I know that I had to come back here from heaven to find my Twin Flame Todd on earth. And to be Todd's Angel here to prepare him for his journey to heaven. And now my beloved Twin Flame Todd is my Angel in heaven guiding me from heaven to help me complete our Twin Flames mission together. God blessed us with three beautiful years together here. And, I know that Todd is now waiting for me to go back home to heaven when I have served and completed my purpose here on earth. And that it is then when we will be together forever eternally for eternity, and one with God.

Chapter 22

Healed By God's Light

It was two weeks since my Todd's passing. I was still inconsolable. Beyond heartbroken, and grieving such an unimaginable loss. What I still couldn't get over was how we really never got to say goodbye. Even though I knew he came to me in my dream and hugged me to reassure me he would always be with me spiritually. A part of me was still broken—my heart was broken. Sometimes, I felt like I was going to die of a broken heart. I just couldn't see past the pain that I was in. My Twin Flame left me so unexpectedly, and the thought of knowing I was never going to see him again in this lifetime was unbearable. I needed to be back in his arms again.

He died on January 15, 2020. On February 1, 2020, a miracle occurred—Todd found his way back into my arms again. I could sense his presence in my bedroom all night before going to sleep. I knew he was there. So, I started talking to him. Telling him how much I loved and missed him. And, how happy I was for him that he was in the most beautiful place you can be in—heaven. I knew how glorious heaven was having been there myself—before being sent back here. I told Todd how much it comforted me knowing that he is waiting for me in heaven, which was confirmed after I asked him for a sign. Which he did with that pair of beautiful white swans, which represented his love and devotion to me.

The promise of him waiting for me. Perhaps that was all I could hope for. I mean what more could I really ask for? I did ask him to come to me in my dream that night. I said, "Please come to me in a loving dream tonight." Then, I played our special song for him—it's called "Could It Be Magic" by Barry Manilow. It was Todd and my song, and we always would listen to it while lying in each other's arms. Todd loved it because the song really reminded him of me. As there was an Angel in the song with my name, and I was Todd's Angel!

After playing that song for him I went to sleep, and did have a dream of Todd. It was a beautiful romantic dream of being intimate with Todd. In my dream I was so happy being back in Todd's arms again. Then all of a sudden I woke from my dream, and something very magical did happen! In the middle of the dream I was woken by the most powerful presence I have ever known. When I opened my eyes I saw God's spirit floating above my bed! And, it kept moving closer towards me. It was a whirling mist with light in the center, and God's glorious spirit kept whirling down closer to me until He was close enough to wrap His arms, which were now pure loving light, around me. His arms had light radiating throughout both arms. God gently wrapped His arms underneath me, and lifted me up pouring all of His magnificent light, love, and healing energy into me— until I felt all of my pain disappearing from every fiber of my being. And, being replaced with pure light, love and healing energy. To say that this was completely miraculous would be an understatement. This was beyond words or comprehension. If I thought I was basking in all of God's glory in heaven, this was even more exquisite!

I felt so much light, love, and healing energy from God's Spirit going into my Spirit, healing me not only from my broken heart of my beloved Todd dying suddenly. But, God was also healing me from any past trauma or pain I had ever gone through in my entire life! Being replaced with the purest spiritual peace and love that I have ever known. It was stronger than any loving moment I had ever had with Todd before he went to heaven. And even stronger than when I stood before God in heaven. It was so powerful and magnificent because all of my sorrow and grief was now gone. God's light and love healed me. He kept His arms around me, which felt like wave upon wave upon waves in the ocean. How strong the current of tides of waves would feel, as it's pulling you out to sea in the strongest riptide. It was the strongest, most powerful surge of love I have ever felt. But, God's embrace was pure light and love—and the energy of Him was so powerful, and magnificent. I knew He was transcending all of His spirit through me. So, that I would know Todd and I are bound by destiny here, and in heaven. I know he is with me now wherever I am, wherever I go, and with every breath that I take. There is no need for me to grieve anymore. Because, my heart is no longer broken. God and Todd's spirit lives on in me forever. His light, and love that I felt in His embrace healed me completely. I can still feel Him hugging me. As I'm writing this, my shoulders and arms where He hugged me have this warm heat where He wrapped His loving arms of light and love around me. I am healed. God is good. I know how much God and Todd love me—their light and love is my light and love. I kept receiving more incredible afterlife communication from Todd, and God.

A few days after my extraordinary encounter of God healing me I was driving home from town when I spotted two beautiful golden retrievers walking past my house on leashes with their owner. I did not know who they were, as I had never seen them in my neighborhood before. I smiled because Todd always had golden retrievers his whole life. He even had two golden retrievers at the time of his death. I started to wonder if these two golden retrievers walking past my house could be a sign from Todd. Just as I thought that I heard Todd say to me, "Turn on your radio." I immediately turned on my car radio and a song began to play. My mouth dropped open because it was the song "(you're the) Best Thing That Ever Happened To Me" by Gladys Knight. I knew Todd dedicated that song to me! I cried out loud to Todd, "You know, Todd, you know that I'm writing our love story!" Because there was a reference to that in the song, and I had just started writing our beautiful spiritual love story in my book, and knew that Todd was letting me know he was aware of it. I cried out again to Todd and said if you're here with me now give me another sign, and he did!

As soon as that song ended, my car shut off by itself! It gave me so much comfort to know my precious Todd knew I was writing our love story. And his extraordinary afterlife communications with me just kept coming. Another time I was driving my daughter to her friend's house when I said to her I will never have that kind of love with any other man again because Todd and my love was so true. As soon as I said our love was so true, a white truck cut in front of my car, and on the back of the truck was one word in big bold letters. It was the word "True"! Even my daughter's mouth dropped open! I said to her, "See, Todd is confirming it! That our love is so True!"

Todd died on January 15, 2020, and a year later on January 5, 2021, Todd called me from heaven. I was talking out loud to Todd saying to him, "Todd, I need you to help me get my manuscript *Hope From Heaven* into the right hands for a movie to be made out of it." As soon as I said it, I heard my phone ring, but did not answer it, because I was in another room. A little later on when I looked at my caller ID to see who called I nearly fainted! I saw that it was Todd who had called me! I screamed out loud! Todd just called me from heaven! On my caller ID was Todd's cell phone number, with the name of a famous Hollywood director, Mikael Hafstrom. I was so amazed because I knew my beloved Todd was letting me know from heaven that this Hollywood director Mikael Hafstrom is the right hands to get my manuscript *Hope From Heaven* into for a movie to be made out of it. Now if I can just convince Mikael Hafstrom that! Somehow I'm sure that Todd will help me to do so from heaven!

Another amazing sign from Todd was I was standing outside of my house talking to some of my neighbors when they commented on how beautiful the leaves were on the ground.

I said to them, yes that fall was always Todd's favorite season because he loved all of the beautiful different colors of leaves. As soon as I said that this strong wind started to blow out of nowhere, and all of these different colors of leaves started blowing, and swirling all around me, and only me! And did not touch the ground. It wasn't even windy out, yet these leaves kept blowing and swirling all around me, making this wonderful swooshing sound. My neighbors were completely in awe of it, as the leaves continued to swirl all around me from all different directions with such force and intensity for about a minute! My neighbors just stood there completely fixated on it, almost as if they were in a trance. They simply could not believe their very eyes! I just smiled and said, "It's my Todd!"

I'm always so happy when Memorial Day Weekend rolls around, as it is the unofficial beginning of summer. All winter long I look forward towards my Cherry Blossom tree blooming (in full bloom), the birds singing, and the boats sailing by. I was particularly delighted when I saw so many birds flying in a frenzy, soaring high and low for more than an hour. Knowing that birds are messengers of spirit, I took two videos of these mystical birds who continued their circling with such intensity throughout the night. It wasn't until I played my videos back that I realized they were reacting to my Angel Todd and God's energy! In my first video the birds were circling around my Angel Todd who was on my grass and in the water. The second video the birds were circling around the spirit of God in the sky. It truly took my breath away! I knew that these were Angel birds sent by God to protect and heal me, to let me know that my Angel Twin Flame Todd and God are always with me, watching over me, loving, guiding and protecting me. It was as if the sky opened up and the spirit of God came down from heaven to me! There was light radiating all around the spirit of God, and the birds were magnificent, too, because birds are messengers of spirit. And there were so many of these mystical birds that came to me from heaven with my Angel Todd and Heavenly Father God.

Two of these magical birds stayed with me, and moved into my garage. They built a bird nest, and their four precious baby birds were born on the 4th of July. I took videos and pictures of these beautiful, mystical birds. They are barn swallow birds, which are said to be God's favorite and holiest birds! They are incredibly special to me. I was sad to see them leave my garage to fly south as the summer was coming to an end. It was thrilling to see the baby barn swallows learn to spread their wings and fly. I blessed all of them, and watched them head south. I prayed they should have a safe flight to warmer weather for the winter, and hoped the mom and dad barn swallows would return to me in the spring. I read that the baby birds leave the nest for good. But, that the mom and dad birds always come back to the same nest each spring.

A couple weeks after they flew south, my daughter had a car accident. A deer darted out in front of her car, before she even had any time to slam on her brakes. The deer unfortunately died. My daughter thankfully was not hurt, but was visibly shaken from the accident. She called me hysterically crying, and kept saying, "I feel so bad the deer died." I told her it was not her fault that the deer ran out in front of her car. She was truly inconsolable because she is as big of an animal lover as I am. And it was just a baby deer, so her heart was broken for the deer. When she came home I could not believe my very eyes. When I went to comfort my daughter as she was walking into the garage, my mouth dropped open! My mystical, magical spiritual barn swallows were in my garage! They were sent back to me to protect my daughter from her car accident! They came back to protect and comfort her, and me too! I burst out into tears when I saw them! They seemed to calm my daughter down too when I said to her, "Look they came back to protect, and comfort you!" The next morning when I woke up they were gone. I smiled knowing my birds, God's holiest barn swallows, flew south again. I eagerly await their returning to me again this spring. I call them my Angel birds!

Todd comes to me all the time in visitation dreams. One of my favorite visitation dreams from Todd was on my daughter's sixteenth birthday. Todd came to me, and I was so happy to see him that I nuzzled my face into the side of his neck and said, "Todd, Todd, I just want to stay with you a little bit longer." Todd smiled sweetly and said, "Look who I brought with me to see you, look who's here." I turned my head from nuzzling into Todd's neck, and I saw my childhood dog Shag, and I was ecstatic to see him! Shag was young, healthy, and full of energy! He kept running around in circles excited to see me! What a treat it was to know my precious dog Shag was visiting me with my beloved Twin Flame Todd on my daughter's birthday! And, for everyone who wonders if their pets go to heaven too, they do! I assure you that you will be reunited with them in heaven one day!

Todd also came to me in a visitation dream a few weeks before my birthday to warn me I was about to suffer from a kidney stones attack. And, when I woke up and stood up to get out of bed, I immediately collapsed in pain, and was rushed to the emergency room where I was diagnosed with having a kidney stones attack! Just as my beloved Twin Flame had warned me about. Thankfully two weeks later on my birthday I was kidney stone free. That was the best birthday present! As anyone who ever had kidney stones knows how painful it is. Some people even say it is more painful then childbirth! I would have to say it's a tie! And, wouldn't want to go through either one again!

Another miraculous sign I received was I was fortunate enough to have received two traditional publishing contracts for my book *Hope From Heaven*. It is very hard to get a traditional publishing contract with a literary agent, and practically impossible without an agent. I decided to do it by myself without a literary agent. I knew how extraordinary my miraculous true story is, and was confident I could receive a book deal on my own. I was very pleased when I was offered a traditional contract by these two wonderful publishers. One was in NYC, and the other was in the UK. They were both equally as good, so the decision was very difficult to make. I decided to let go and let God. Before going to sleep the night before New Year's Eve, I prayed to God to send me a sign as to which publisher is best for me to sign a contract with. This was one decision I needed to put in God's hands. Sure enough God heard my call for him, and answered my prayer. When I fell asleep I had a dream and in my dream I was told that I should sign my book publishing contract with the UK publisher John Hunt Publishing/O-Books because O-Books is their spiritual imprint, and they are the perfect genre for my book.

When I woke up early the next morning I felt that was my sign from God to go with O-Books. Just as I was thinking that, my cell phone rang, and I said to myself who is calling me so early in the morning? It was 6:48am. I picked up my iPhone and saw it was a FaceTime call from one of O-Books' authors. I said to myself, why is Colm calling me this early? I figured it must be important so I answered my phone but the call got disconnected. Which sometimes happens due to not getting good Wi-Fi reception throughout my whole house. I immediately e-mailed Colm, and said I'm going to another part of my house where I get better Wi-Fi reception. I told him to FaceTime me again in ten minutes. Twenty minutes went by, and Colm did not FaceTime me back. Then my iPhone pinged, and I saw I got a text message from Colm, but a strange message that said, "Mmm." I thought, that is not something that Colm would say! And, my intuition told me that it wasn't Colm who FaceTimed me, or texted me, I knew it had to be God and Todd making contact with me from heaven! I immediately texted Colm back and said, "Did you FaceTime me and send me this text message?" I also e-mailed him to kindly let me know as soon as possible because if it wasn't him then I knew God was answering my prayer letting me know I should definitely sign my book contract with John Hunt Publishing/O-Books.

It was New Year's Eve, and Colm must have been celebrating the New Year because he did not reply until two days later. I was certain he did not FaceTime or text me being that he was taking so long to respond to me. And sure enough on January 2, 2022 finally I received an e-mail from Colm saying, "No I didn't xx." I was so happy, as if a huge weight was lifted off my shoulders, because God answered my prayer of letting me know which book publisher was best for me to go with, by sending me His amazing signs through this FaceTime call and text message from O-Books author Colm Holland to me, to reassure me that I am destined to sign my book publishing contract with O-Books. I didn't need any more convincing—between my dream to sign my contract with O-Books and my FaceTime call and text message from Colm Holland, which he did neither—that it was God, and I would also like to think Todd was who FaceTimed and texted me.

I signed my contract with John Hunt Publishing/O-Books with total peace and clarity. I thanked God for guiding me in the right direction, and promised Him I will do everything that I can to make Him proud of me, to serve and complete my purpose for Him to enlighten everyone all over the world all about God's light and love, spirituality and purpose here on earth as well as in heaven through this book *Hope From Heaven*.

I truly feel blessed that I have not only met God in heaven, but that His spirit came down to earth two times to me. I spoke to a priest and a rabbi, who confirmed my video and picture are of God's Spirit. Then I asked them, "Why was I the chosen one?" They said I have been blessed, and no one knows why God chooses who He does to be His messenger for Him here on earth. My answer to that is God Only Knows! I am just honored to do some of His spiritual work for Him here on earth.

Epilogue

Today is my beloved Todd's birthday, August 31st. He would have been sixty-six years old. He continues to send me miraculous signs from heaven every day. He sent me a particularly meaningful one on his birthday this morning. I was watching the sun rise, one of my favorite things to do because I always see the beauty of Todd's spirit in the light of every new dawn. As I was standing by my patio door admiring the particularly glorious sunrise, I was filled with emotion thinking how I wish my darling twin soul Todd was here with me physically to celebrate his birthday with him. Then all of a sudden I heard a loud bang, and when I looked I saw a big, beautiful bird had slammed into my patio glass door and died. Normally I would have been so upset for the poor bird. But, I knew it was a beautiful sign from Todd on his birthday. And this was no ordinary bird, it was a gorgeous belted kingfisher. I have never seen one where I live, and it was a message from Todd that he is always with me. I know that birds deliver significant messages during the birthdays of people close to you that have already passed away. I immediately took a picture of it just as I took photos of the magnificent pair of swans that Todd sent me on the morning of his funeral. That conveyed the message to me that we are Twin Flames, and they represent the energy of unconditional love and Twin Flame Union. The eternal love of oneness between two beings. Little did I know that my Prince Charming was really my Twin Flame all along!

What started out as a teenage celebrity crush turned into true love. When Todd and I fell deeply in love, we thought we were soul mates. It was Todd who let me know from heaven that we are really Twin Flames. Then he sent me the beautiful pair of swans on the morning of his funeral. A pair of swans are the Twin Flames spirit animal, and represent the eternal love of oneness between two beings. Twin Flames are one soul that was split into two bodies and share the same consciousness. You can have many soul mates, but only one Twin Flame, because it is the other half of your soul. They are very empathetic ascended masters. They knew their journey before entering this earth.

Before I met Todd, I started having the same reoccurring dream of him marrying me. In my dream my mom was always walking me down the aisle where Todd was waiting for me at the altar. Then I would always wake up from my dream. I stopped having the dream during the time that Todd and I were together, and as soon as Todd died I started having that same dream again. That is another confirmation to me that Todd and I are Twin Flames, as very often you dream about your Twin Flame before you meet each other. Twin Flame union is two people coming together by the hand of the divine.

It is important because of the big love that two Twin Flames coming together creates. When Twin Flames come together a huge beam of light shines onto the world. It is the unconditional love this planet is ascending towards. When Twin Flames become one they naturally align the planet to more unity and divinity. Twin Flame union is important for the ascension of this planet. Eventually the Twin Flames will merge back into the one soul that they were before the split into the two twin souls. The early stages of this reunion usually happens in both of their last lifetimes on the planet so they can complete the Ascension process together.

You only meet your Twin Flame in your last lifetime when your soul is very advanced because you are sent here as light workers. That is why Todd was a wonderful therapist, as well as the founder of a suicide prevention clinic. And why God sent me back here as his messenger to spread his light and love throughout the world. I know Todd is waiting to marry me in heaven, as the Twin Flame connection is the ultimate Alchemical Marriage. Todd already let me know when he came to me in a visitation dream that he is waiting for me in heaven. That once

God calls me back home, each half of Todd and my soul will merge as one again, where we will be one with God for all of eternity. As Plato wrote, "and when one of them meets the other half, the actual half of himself, whether he be a lover of youth, or a lover of another sort, the pair are lost in an amazement of love and friendship and intimacy and one will not be out of each other's sight as I may say, even for a moment."

It is my wish that *Hope From Heaven* inspired you that God truly does exist in heaven, having stood before Him myself, and being sent back as His messenger, and light worker. And, comfort you that your loved ones in heaven are always with you spiritually because your soul is eternal, and true love never dies, it is endless...

To see Elissa's fascinating afterlife communication from Todd and God, please visit Elissa Hope's YouTube channel. Kindly like it, share it, leave a comment and subscribe.

To connect with Elissa Hope, or for film rights to her book, visit her author website at www.elissahope.com.

O-BOOKS

SPIRITUALITY

O is a symbol of the world, of oneness and unity; this eye represents knowledge and insight. We publish titles on general spirituality and living a spiritual life. We aim to inform and help you on your own journey in this life.

If you have enjoyed this book, why not tell other readers by posting a review on your preferred book site?

The Holy Spirit's Interpretation of the New Testament
A Course in Understanding and Acceptance
Regina Dawn Akers
Following on from the strength of *A Course In Miracles*, NTI
teaches us how to experience the love and oneness of God.
Paperback: 978-1-84694-085-9 ebook: 978-1-78099-083-5

The Message of A Course In Miracles
A translation of the Text in plain language
Elizabeth A. Cronkhite
A translation of *A Course in Miracles* into plain, everyday
language for anyone seeking inner peace. The companion
volume, *Practicing A Course In Miracles*, offers practical lessons
and mentoring.
Paperback: 978-1-84694-319-5 ebook: 978-1-84694-642-4

Your Simple Path
Find Happiness in every step
Ian Tucker
A guide to helping us reconnect with what is really important in
our lives.
Paperback: 978-1-78279-349-6 ebook: 978-1-78279-348-9

365 Days of Wisdom
Daily Messages To Inspire You Through The Year
Dadi Janki
Daily messages which cool the mind, warm the heart and guide
you along your journey.
Paperback: 978-1-84694-863-3 ebook: 978-1-84694-864-0

Body of Wisdom
Women's Spiritual Power and How it Serves
Hilary Hart
Bringing together the dreams and experiences of women across
the world with today's most visionary spiritual teachers.
Paperback: 978-1-78099-696-7 ebook: 978-1-78099-695-0

Dying to Be Free
From Enforced Secrecy to Near Death to True Transformation
Hannah Robinson
After an unexpected accident and near-death experience, Hannah
Robinson found herself radically transforming her life, while a
remarkable new insight altered her relationship with her father, a
practising Catholic priest.
Paperback: 978-1-78535-254-6 ebook: 978-1-78535-255-3

The Ecology of the Soul
A Manual of Peace, Power and Personal Growth for Real People
in the Real World
Aidan Walker
Balance your own inner Ecology of the Soul to regain your
natural state of peace, power and wellbeing.
Paperback: 978-1-78279-850-7 ebook: 978-1-78279-849-1

Not I, Not other than I
The Life and Teachings of Russel Williams
Steve Taylor, Russel Williams
The miraculous life and inspiring teachings of one of the World's
greatest living Sages.
Paperback: 978-1-78279-729-6 ebook: 978-1-78279-728-9

On the Other Side of Love
A woman's unconventional journey towards wisdom
Muriel Maufroy
When life has lost all meaning, what do you do?
Paperback: 978-1-78535-281-2 ebook: 978-1-78535-282-9

Practicing A Course In Miracles
A translation of the Workbook in plain language, with
mentor's notes
Elizabeth A. Cronkhite
The practical second and third volumes of The Plain-Language
A Course In Miracles.
Paperback: 978-1-84694-403-1 ebook: 978-1-78099-072-9

Quantum Bliss
The Quantum Mechanics of Happiness, Abundance, and Health
George S. Mentz
Quantum Bliss is the breakthrough summary of success and
spirituality secrets that customers have been waiting for.
Paperback: 978-1-78535-203-4 ebook: 978-1-78535-204-1

The Upside Down Mountain
Mags MacKean
A must-read for anyone weary of chasing success and happiness
– one woman's inspirational journey swapping the uphill slog for
the downhill slope.
Paperback: 978-1-78535-171-6 ebook: 978-1-78535-172-3

Your Personal Tuning Fork
The Endocrine System
Deborah Bates
Discover your body's health secret, the endocrine system, and
'twang' your way to sustainable health!
Paperback: 978-1-84694-503-8 ebook: 978-1-78099-697-4

Readers of ebooks can buy or view any of these bestsellers by clicking on the live link in the title. Most titles are published in paperback and as an ebook. Paperbacks are available in traditional bookshops. Both print and ebook formats are available online.
Find more titles and sign up to our readers' newsletter at http://www.johnhuntpublishing.com/mind-body-spirit
Follow us on Facebook at https://www.facebook.com/OBooks/
and Twitter at https://twitter.com/obooks